CW01091586

FIRST IN, LAST OUT

First In, Last Out

The Post-War Organisation, Employment
and Training of Royal Marines Commandos

EDITED BY PAUL WINTER

CASEMATE

Oxford & Philadelphia

Published in Great Britain and the United States of America in 2021 by
CASEMATE PUBLISHERS
The Old Music Hall, 106–108 Cowley Road, Oxford OX4 1JE, UK
and
1950 Lawrence Road, Havertown, PA 19083, USA

Copyright 2021 © Paul Winter

Hardcover Edition: ISBN 978-1-61200-962-9
Digital Edition: ISBN 978-1-61200-963-6

A CIP record for this book is available from the British Library

All rights reserved. No part of this book may be reproduced or transmitted in any form or by
any means, electronic or mechanical including photocopying, recording or by any information
storage and retrieval system, without permission from the publisher in writing.

Printed and bound in the United Kingdom by TJ Books

For a complete list of Casemate titles, please contact:

CASEMATE PUBLISHERS (UK)
Telephone (01865) 241249
Email: casemate-uk@casematepublishers.co.uk
www.casematepublishers.co.uk

CASEMATE PUBLISHERS (US)
Telephone (610) 853-9131
Fax (610) 853-9146
Email: casemate@casematepublishers.com
www.casematepublishers.com

The information in this book is reproduced for study only. The publisher assumes no responsibility
of liability of any damage incurred resulting from following any of the instructions printed in
this book.

First In, Last Out is dedicated to the memory of
Stan "Scotty" Scott (1924–2014),
member of 3 Troop, No. 3 Commando;
Chairman of the Commando Veterans' Association;
mentor to generations of Army Cadets;
and exemplar of the "Commando Spirit".

Contents

Foreword

"To see where we are going, we must know where we are, and to know where are, we must discover how we got here."

General Sir John "Shan" Hackett

The statement above by that battle-wise soldier, "Shan" Hackett, and repeated by the author Paul Winter at the end of his introduction, is the clue to what *First In, Last Out* is about. Paul Winter uses an unpublished pamphlet, *Amphibious Warfare Handbook No. 10a: The Organisation, Employment and Training of Commandos, 1951*, as a starting point from which to examine where the Royal Marines are now, and how they got there. He tells us that this pamphlet, a "unique example of bespoke Royal Marines Commando doctrine (intended to be read in conjunction with *Amphibious Warfare Handbook No. 10b: Amphibious Raids, 1951*), has escaped the full attention of both practitioners and scholars."

He then goes on to ask what *Amphibious Warfare Handbook No. 10a* consists of, when was it produced, by whom, why was it written and for whom? What was the historical context, and does it have any relevance for today's Royal Marines and the new Future Commando Force (FCF) concept?

I believe it has significant relevance. The Royal Marines today are going through a period in their existence best summed up by saying "we have been here before many times." Usually because there is uncertainty and doubt among those responsible for the defence policy of the United Kingdom, and especially at the top of the naval service, about what the Royal Marines are for; indeed why they exist at all. Those who compiled *Amphibious Warfare Handbook No. 10a* had recently and personally taken part in the war against Germany and the Axis powers. This, in the words of Paul Winter, "gave this doctrinal paper credibility largely absent in doctrine generated during prolonged periods of peace." He might have added after long periods without war against a peer enemy, as pertains today. He goes on to quote John Gooch, a military historian:

> The basic problem is that military organizations can rarely replicate in times of peace the actual conditions of war. It becomes increasingly easy as the complexities, ambiguities and frictions of combat recede into the past, for militaries to develop concepts, and practices that meet the standards of peacetime efficiency rather than those of wartime effectiveness.

Furthermore, Paul Winter identifies later in his introduction that at present, rather than the exigencies of war dictating the Concept of Employment (CONEMP) for Commandos, design models constructed in peacetime may be forced upon them. These models may be based on a desire to save money, or on one particular scenario because it fits the defence mood of the time; a model that lacks flexibility and the ability to react to the actual circumstances; one constructed in the minds of those reacting to pressures other than the actual enemy threat. This is a style of thinking that was criticized by a former Commandant General Royal Marines (CGRM) who remarked; "The truth is that you have to wage war as you can and not necessarily as you would like to."

Ever since the end of World War II the Royal Marines have operated in exactly the same way as that proscribed by General Sir Anthony Farrar-Hockley describing his own regiment, The Parachute Regiment, like the Royal Marines elite and frequently under threat of cuts and even total oblivion: "It was a regiment for all seasons, or it was nothing. It must take on whatever task it is given and do its best at it." The Royal Marines likewise cannot afford the luxury of pre-selecting which tactical or operational tasks they will, or will not undertake, or the self-indulgence of placing provisos on the scale and manner of their future employment.

The example of 41 Commando RM in Korea provides a case study in the dangers of inflexibility caused by designing a force for just one role. Paul Winter reminds us that this experience "spotlights the numerous potential pitfalls for the FCF, for not only does it address the dangers of 'mission creep', re-roling mid-campaign, deficiencies in mass, the dislocation of expectation and the critical importance of inter-operability; it also illustrates the hazards of over-specialisation and sub-optimal force configurations."

41 Commando RM, at less than half the strength of a "normal" RM Commando of the period, was sent to Korea to operate as a raiding force. It did so successfully, but as the US-led United Nations force pushed back the North Koreans and closed up to the border with China, there was little coastline left to raid and 41 Commando found itself out of a job. The Commanding Officer, Lieutenant Colonel Drysdale, eventually persuaded Major-General O. P. Smith, commanding the 1st US Marine Division, to request that 41 Commando join his division in their advance north from Hungnam to the Chosin Reservoir. Having fought its way up to join the 1st US Marine Division, there followed the desperate battles at Hagaru-ri and "Hell Fire Valley" against the newly arrived Chinese People's Liberation Army, who had intervened in the war in October 1950. As a mobile reserve, 41 Commando rendered gallant service covering the withdrawal of Smith's division, fighting its way out – the legendary march to the sea, in the process battling through and breaking contact with at least four Chinese divisions. The Commando was later awarded the US Presidential Citation, but from an initial strength of around 250 all ranks was now down to just 150. Plans to attach 41 Commando to the 1st US Marine Division now operating in the line as normal infantry came to naught, as the Commando was not configured for, or sufficiently strong enough to operate, in this way – for despite receiving reinforcements rifle troops were a mere 45 all ranks.

41 Commando was then deployed to the Wonsan harbour area and the neighbouring islands for raiding. Here it was misemployed thanks to coalition politics, and brushes with US intelligence organisations, which treated the Commando as rivals. Despite these difficulties since their arrival in Korea, by the time 41 Commando was disbanded in February 1952, they had carried out numerous successful raids and cut the enemy's communications, as well as operating as "normal" infantry supporting the 1st US Marine Division in the battles around Hagaru-ri and the march to the sea. But fighting in the line in the static warfare that occurred later in Korea was not a sensible option; 41 Commando was not organised and lacked the manpower to undertake such a commitment.

The point is that Royal Marines trained as infantry, and organised as such, can seamlessly segue from raiding to fighting as normal infantry, and back again – the proviso being if they are organised and trained as such. You do not need to have a special organisation for a 750-strong Commando of three or four rifle companies to be able to raid. Raids can be at section, troop, company, or even Commando level. Equally, you should not commit a 250-strong unit formed into some esoteric set up, and purely trained in special tasks, to "normal" infantry fighting.

Those who wish to return the Royal Marines to their "Commando roots" are perhaps allowing an element of romanticism to overrule facts. The original Commandos contained a sizeable proportion of officers who were not infantrymen by training; hence opting for troops rather than companies. The troop organisation is not suitable for conventional infantry fighting, as it is not divisible into three platoon-size sub-units; just two. Paul Winter's introduction discusses these aspects and why the Royal Marines changed to a company system in 1961; and not before time as many of us who were serving then thought.

Of the 38 World War II battle honours listed on the Commando Memorial in Westminster Abbey, a mere four commemorate raids. Of those, the Royal Marines participated in just one – Dieppe: a disaster not attributable to the Royal Marines involved. The other 34 commemorate main force engagements in which Commandos played a distinguished part fighting as infantry carrying out difficult tasks, which they fulfilled brilliantly. The action at Port-en-Bessin by 47 (RM) Commando on the right flank of the British sector of the Normandy beachhead is a shining example.

There is indeed much to learn from *Amphibious Warfare Handbook No. 10a* and from Paul Winter's introduction. Both merit study and reflection. As an indication of how it was unknown in the Royal Marines, I joined in 1952, served for 34 years, and am now president of the Royal Marines Historical Society, and until Paul Winter brought it to my attention, I was totally unaware of the existence of *Amphibious Warfare Handbook No. 10a*.

Major-General Julian Thompson CB OBE RM,
Commander of 3 Commando Brigade
during the 1982 Falklands War

Acknowledgements

First of all, I would like to thank my friend and colleague, Colonel Paul Maynard OBE RM, for making this project possible. Without his conceptual awareness, moral courage and far-sightedness, I would never have had the honour of providing academic support to the Royal Marines. I also wish to acknowledge the assistance of Major-General Julian Thompson RM (retired) for casting his critical eye over my work and for kindly supplying a foreword. It is much appreciated. Thanks must also go to Lieutenant-Colonel Tom Quinn RM, CSM Tony Wilson RM (retired), Major Lee Stewart RM, Colonel Ollie Lee OBE RM (retired), WO2 Lee Cullen RM, and Mr John Rawlinson. All devoted their time and energy in assisting me with my research.

In particular, I would like to thank Lieutenant-Colonel Tom Noble RM whose eagle eyes spotted *Amphibious Warfare Handbook No. 10a* languishing on a bookshelf in the doctrinal depository of the Hobson Library, an integral part of the UK Defence Academy, Shrivenham. I am in his debt.

Further gratitude must go to Mr Luke Johnstone, Advanced Command and Staff Course Liaison Librarian at the Hobson Library, and his staff for all their assistance. Without their patience and generosity this project would have been a hundred times harder to complete.

As the in-house academic at 40 Commando Royal Marines from 2017 to 2020, I wish to pay tribute to the incredible Officers, Warrant Officers, NCOs and Marines of the unit who made me feel so welcome, and who listened to what little advice and guidance I could offer such fiercely professional fighting men. It was an absolute privilege and a pleasure to be associated with such a first-class organisation.

Mrs Ruth Sheppard and the team at Casemate Publishers also need to be recognised for their faith in the book, as well as all the assistance, advice and support they delivered throughout the book's gestation period. It was an absolute pleasure to publish with them.

Finally, I could not have published *The Organisation, Employment and Training of Commandos, 1951* without the love, support and understanding of my wife, whose unstinting belief in my work made this publication possible. I would also like to express my indebtedness to my parents-in-law, Michael and Susan Moberly, for all their help over the years, and to my son, who is a constant source of joy in my life. Thank you all.

Introduction

"... the future is best built on good things which have emerged from the past."

Brigadier The Lord Lovat, 1978[1]

Erroneously referred to in the "definitive" history of the wartime Commandos as *Commando Training Notes, 1953*[2] and recently in the Royal Marines' own Corps journal, *The Globe & Laurel*, as the *Affirmation of Royal Marines Commandos, 1952*,[3] *Amphibious Warfare Handbook No. 10a: The Organisation, Employment and Training of Commandos, 1951* has never before been published or quoted at length. Held at The National Archives (TNA) Kew, under catalogue reference DEFE 2/1770,[4] the true significance of this unique example of bespoke Royal Marines Commando doctrine, (intended to be read in conjunction with *Amphibious Warfare Handbook No. 10b: Amphibious Raids, 1951*),[5] has curiously escaped the full attention of practitioners and scholars alike.[6] This is despite the fact that the year 2021 marks the 70th anniversary of its official publication.

The obscurity of this primary source to a 21st-century audience therefore obliges the historian to pose certain questions as to its existence, specifically: what is *Amphibious Warfare Handbook No. 10a: The Organisation, Employment and Training of Commandos, 1951*? What does it consist of? When was it produced and by whom? Why was it written and for what type of audience? What was the historical context to this doctrinal document? And what relevance, if any, does it have for today's Royal Marines and the new Future Commando Force (FCF) concept?

No less important are a set of supplementary questions, namely, "what kind of institutional need was [this] particular doctrine a response to?

What was the institutional context? Where did the doctrine makers 'come from'? i.e. what kind of personal and institutional experience did they have, and where were they heading? [And] [w]hat were their main political and military concerns?"[7]

What is the Handbook and What Does it Consist of?

Classified "confidential", as opposed to the higher security classifications "secret" and "top secret", this sensitive official document was nevertheless not intended for wide circulation. Nor was it designed, moreover, for "Public Relations purposes", or "tailor-made for spectators and bystanders".[8] In sharp contrast to the 21st century, where "fourth generation doctrine" is produced for marketing and propaganda means, and is therefore accessible to a wide audience,[9] in 1951 members of the British general public simply could not walk into their nearest branch of His Majesty's Stationery Office (HMSO) and purchase a copy.

At the heart of this official sensitivity to unauthorised disclosure was the "… generic paradox of all doctrines", namely, "how to make them useful to us, but not to our enemies".[10] With the very real threat in 1951 that the nascent Cold War could turn "hot" at any moment, it was imperative that such defence-related material did not fall into the hands of Stalin's agents.[11] Consequently, when "not in actual use", *Amphibious Warfare Handbook No. 10a* was to be kept under "lock and key", with the "officer or official in possession of this document" being "responsible for its safe custody" and that its "contents [were] not [to be] disclosed to any unauthorised person".[12]

Security precautions aside, *Amphibious Warfare Handbook No. 10a* is a self-avowed piece of dedicated Royal Marines Commando "doctrine", produced to meet the emerging defence requirements of the post-war world. As much is attested to at the end of the handbook's contents page where the term "doctrine" is clearly written. Historically, this is significant, for the British Army engendered the impression in 1989 that it was the "doctrinal avant-garde in Britain",[13] having published *Design for Military Operations: The British Military Doctrine*,[14] which was declared to be "breaking new ground" by being the "first articulated doctrine at a level above the tactical".[15] But what exactly is doctrine and what is its function?

Doctrine

There exists a general consensus that doctrine is a manifestation of a military organisation's "collective wisdom", a mixture of history, experience and practice, augmented by theory and experimentation. It is a bridge between thought and practice; it standardises terminology; and is a detailed guide to action and "best practice". Quite simply, doctrine is "considered thought on the best way of doing things".[16] Yet one leading expert on military doctrine has confessed that as "there is no commonly recognised definition of doctrine ...", a necessity therefore exists to "figure out what doctrine actually *is* in order to be in a position to look at its nature and character".[17]

To this end, the same authority opined that it is highly advisable to differentiate between "doctrines on one side and half-breed doctrines and other written documents used by the military to facilitate operations on the other ..."[18], for if doctrine is "reduced to a military how-to-do guide or a catalogue of cunning tricks of the trade", it can "no longer" be treated as "doctrine", but rather as a military "manual or handbook".[19]

In light of these distinctions, *Amphibious Warfare Handbook No. 10a* may be classified as a "half-breed" piece of doctrine, for it is, in essence, a hybrid. On the one hand it conforms to a definition of doctrine imprimaturised by leading military scholars, namely a document that contains "an approved set of principles and methods, intended to provide large military organisations with a common outlook and a uniform basis of action."[20] But on the other, it serves as a "how-to-do guide", as well as providing its readership with a "catalogue of cunning tricks of the trade".

With respect to its primary function, "service doctrine", in the opinion of one leading scholar, "explains the goals, identifies the tasks, and shapes the tools of [a military] organisation".[21] It executes this task for three "distinct audiences", specifically, "members of the organisation", "sister military services", and "policymakers";[22] and for three "distinct reasons":

> Directed at organisational members, doctrine helps a military organisation to maintain internal cohesion in how it prepares for, and prosecutes, military operations. Directed at sister services, doctrine facilitates joint and combined operations. Directed at policymakers, doctrine enables a military organisation to maximize its autonomy and resource-base.[23]

Narrowing the focus on functionality still further, official documents such as *Amphibious Warfare Handbook No. 10a* aim to communicate, to an in-house, tribal audience, the following messages: (i) what the military organisation perceives itself to be: "who are we"?; (ii) what its *raison d'être* is: "what do we do"?; (iii) how it carries out its missions: "how do we do that"?; and (iv) historically, how the mission has been carried out: "how did we do that in the past"?[24]

As already noted, past experience is critical to the development of sound doctrine, for a military organisation possessed of a sub-optimal institutional memory will inevitably produce flawed and distorted doctrinal thinking. Fortunately for the Corps, institutional memories of World War II; the costly lessons learned during this global conflict; and the skills, procedures and tactics employed by Commando Forces to help facilitate the defeat of Nazi Germany and the Axis powers, were still fresh in the minds of those who compiled *Amphibious Warfare Handbook No. 10a*.

Importantly, the existence of a strong collective historical consciousness within the Royal Marines afforded this doctrinal paper credibility largely absent in doctrine generated during prolonged periods of peace.[25] This last point was seized upon by one military historian, who reflected:

> The basic problem is that military organizations can rarely replicate in times of peace the actual conditions of war. It becomes increasingly easy as the complexities, ambiguities, and frictions of combat recede into the past, for militaries to develop concepts, doctrines, and practices that meet the standards of peacetime efficiency rather than those of wartime effectiveness.[26]

Luckily for Britain's "sea soldiers", the authors of *Amphibious Warfare Handbook No. 10a* avoided this conceptual pitfall, producing instead "effective doctrine" which was "accessible, credible and relevant" to the period of time in which it was written.[27]

Aside from explaining to the uninitiated how Commandos were to be organised, employed on military operations and trained to successfully execute such operations, this 70-page *aide memoiré* offered its readership further advice and guidance regarding the specialist nature of Royal Marines Commandos. Highlighting the distinctive character of this elite force, the handbook's authors were at pains to emphasise that, "Such doctrine ... must be fully understood by those who are required to adapt it to the special problems of commando warfare", adding that information contained in the "standard infantry and amphibious manuals" of the period would not be repeated in this customized booklet.[28]

Consequently, specialist capabilities and expertises such as amphibious warfare, small and large-scale raiding, the seizure of ports and other strategically important objectives, cliff assaults, sabotage, the hardening of Commando troops for warfare, intelligence-gathering, Commando training, specialized infantry work, guerrilla warfare and Commando tactics were all thoroughly covered.

Eschewing dogma, *Amphibious Warfare Handbook No. 10a* was a detailed guide to "best practice" for Commando soldiers. Stressing the need to maintain professional standards and competencies by means of a variety of specialized skill-sets, it not only presented its audience with a delineation of the characteristics and qualities required of a post-war Royal Marine, but an invaluable insight into the mind-set, *esprit de corps* and ethos of a Commando soldier.

Notably, *Amphibious Warfare Handbooks Nos. 10a* and *10b* were constituent parts of a Confidential Reference Book (CB(R)) series issued by Combined Operations Headquarters (COHQ) and its successor, Headquarters Amphibious Warfare, between 1945 and 1956. The series included Naval Communications in amphibious warfare; naval planning; the employment of air forces; the role of the battalion plus supporting arms; the employment of amphibians and maintenance operations; air defence, air support and naval bombardment; beach intelligence; Combined Operations planning; Royal Engineers, Royal Army Service Corps, Royal Electrical and Mechanical Engineers and Royal Army Ordnance Corps units for beach maintenance and transportation; RAF beach squadrons; and navigational aspects of amphibious warfare.[29]

The Creation of the Handbook

The Directorate of Combined Operations, the first British organisation to possess an inter-service headquarters,[30] was first formed in June 1940 under the direction of the Adjutant General of the Royal Marines, Lieutenant-General A. G. B. Bourne.[31] Its "primary function" was to "train officers and men of the Royal Navy and the Royal Marines, the Army and the Royal Air Force in the conduct of amphibious warfare." Its secondary purpose was to "plan and execute all kinds of raids, small or large."[32] From July 1940 until June 1947 Combined Operations Headquarters was commanded by a succession of highly distinguished directors, advisors and chiefs, namely, Admiral of the Fleet, Lord Keyes (July 1940–October 1941); Lord Louis Mountbatten (October 1941–September 1943); and Major-General Robert Laycock (October 1943–June 1947).[33]

Yet from 1947 until 1951, a series of bureaucratic and departmental changes to COHQ occurred. Although it was decided that COHQ should "continue to be responsible for policy, training and technique in amphibious warfare under the direction of the Chiefs of Staff [CoS]", "responsibility for Combined Operations estimates" was eventually transferred from "the Service ministries to the newly established Ministry of Defence [MoD]". Subsequently, on 1 April 1948, COHQ was "placed under the administration" of the MoD.[34]

Named the Ministry of Defence Combined Operations Headquarters, it wasn't until February 1951, however, that a further alteration to its nomenclature was enacted. According to the seminal text on the role of amphibious warfare in post-war British defence policy, prior to February 1951 the term "amphibious warfare" had not been officially employed by Britain's armed forces, who had hitherto referred to this specialised "mode of warfare" as "combined operations".[35]

Re-titled Amphibious Warfare Headquarters (AWHQ), the old COHQ ceased to exist, and with it its chief who had only recently been re-designated "Chief of Combined Operations Staff". Henceforth, the senior officer responsible for the UK's amphibious capability would be termed "Chief of Amphibious Warfare (CAW)".[36] Notably, Amphibious Warfare HQ was responsible for all specialist doctrine pertaining to the UK's amphibious forces until it was replaced in 1962 by the Joint Warfare Committee, comprising senior representatives of all three services.[37]

Helpfully, this somewhat frenetic refashioning of official titles grants the historian a vital clue as to roughly when in 1951 *The Organisation, Employment and Training of Commandos* was first issued and circulated throughout the Admiralty and War Office. On the front cover of *Amphibious Warfare Handbook No. 10a*, in bold capital letters, it states that this doctrinal pamphlet was, "Prepared under the direction of the Chief of Amphibious Warfare and the Commandant General Royal Marines". Bearing in mind that the appellation Chief of Combined Operations (CCO) was changed to CAW in February of 1951, we know for certain that *The Organisation, Employment and Training of Commandos, 1951* was produced sometime following this pivotal month.

With regards the preparation of this piece of Commando doctrine, it is significant that from June 1947 onwards the post of Chief of Combined Operations/Amphibious Warfare was held by a succession of Royal Marines officers: Major-General G. E. Wildman-Lushington RM (1947–1950), Major-General V. D. Thomas RM (1950–1954), Major-General C. F. Phillips RM (1954–1957),[38] and Major-General Jim Moulton RM (1957–1961).[39] It was to be under the direction of Major-General Vivian Davenport Thomas, however, that *Amphibious Warfare Handbook No. 10a* reached fruition.

Born in October 1897, V. D. Thomas joined the Royal Marines in 1915 and was subsequently posted to the Royal Marines Artillery. Promoted lieutenant in 1916, he joined the battle cruiser HMS *Princess Royal* which saw action at the battle of Jutland in May of that year. Holding a series of sea and shore postings during the inter-war years, Thomas was to occupy a number of key posts during the early stages of World War II, namely, GSO(I) Mobile Naval Base Defence Organisation (MNBDO) from January 1941 to April 1943, and Commander 1st Royal Marine Anti-Aircraft Brigade, from April 1943 until November 1943.[40]

Described in his *Globe & Laurel* obituary as "tall, fit, and imposing, and ... every inch a Blue Marine", Thomas was, nevertheless, a "fair" officer whose "strict" persona meant it "took a little time to detect the twinkle in the eyes behind the fierce moustache and the harsh bark."[41] It wasn't until December 1943, however, that Thomas, now a brigadier, left behind the world of the "Blue Marine" and entered that of Combined Operations and Commando Forces becoming Chief of Staff to the CCO, Bob Laycock, in December 1943.

In September 1946, Thomas was promoted acting major-general and appointed Chief of Staff to the Commandant General Royal Marines (CGRM), a post he held until May 1950. By then a full major-general, Thomas was selected to become Chief of Combined Operations Staff in October 1950, a post whose title, as has already been noted, was restyled Chief of Amphibious Warfare in February 1951. Thomas remained CAW until May 1954, relinquishing the role to Major-General C. F. Phillips.[42]

The other *dramatis persona* behind the preparation of *The Organisation, Employment and Training of Commandos 1951* was General Sir Leslie Hollis RM, the then CGRM. Born in 1897, Hollis, like Vivian Thomas, was a veteran of World War I having joined the Royal Marines Light Infantry (RMLI) in April 1915. Again, like Thomas, Hollis had been present at the battle of Jutland, serving aboard the cruiser HMS *Edinburgh*. Having filled a variety of inter-war postings, he was appointed in 1932 to the plans division of the Admiralty. Recruited thereafter by Sir Maurice Hankey, another Royal Marines officer, who was Secretary to the Cabinet and Committee of Imperial Defence (CID), Hollis was selected as Secretary to the Joint Planning Sub-committee in 1936.[43]

Yet it was to be in his wartime capacity as Secretary to the Defence Committee and Chiefs of Staff Committee, as well as deputy to General Sir Hastings "Pug" Ismay, Chief Staff Officer to the Prime Minister, Winston Churchill, that Hollis discovered his true *métier*. Full of "commonsense, loyal, reliable, calm, imperturbable ... hardworking, cheerful, and unflurried",[44] he later estimated that during the war he had attended 6,000 meetings of the Chiefs of Staff Committee, as well as innumerable meetings of the War Cabinet Defence Committee and numerous inter-Allied conferences.[45]

Hollis's extensive wartime experience of top-level staff work, augmented by a spell as Chief Staff Officer to the Ministry of Defence and Deputy Secretary (Military) between 1946 and 1949, therefore made him a Whitehall operator *par excellence*. Vitally, this in-depth knowledge of, and feel for, the labyrinthine "ways of Whitehall" were to be of inestimable value in ensuring the survival of the Royal Marines Commandos during the next few years of post-war readjustment.

Succeeding General Sir Dallas Brooks RM as CGRM in May 1949, Hollis was immediately faced with a "crisis", for it was a "time of most severe retrenchment in all the defence services".[46] Regrettably, the newly established Royal Marines Commandos were to be no exception. It is perhaps not surprising, therefore, that on being offered the post of CGRM in September 1948, Hollis hesitated. Although possessed of an "immense pride in and love for his corps ...",[47] he had, in his own opinion, "been away from the Corps for thirteen years"; drastic cuts threatened its very future; and one of his best friends had, for some time, been "schooled" to take up the post.

On this last point, Hollis reasoned it would have been an "act of bad faith" to have accepted the professional headship of the Corps over his contemporary.[48] Yet luckily for the Corps, Hollis put aside these personal reservations. Armed with his wartime experience and highly placed connections, as well as adept at playing the Whitehall game,[49] Hollis was the perfect figure to steer the Royal Marines Commandos through the rapids of stringent defence cuts.

Hollis's greatest test on becoming CGRM was to counter and reverse the recommendations of the 1948 Harwood Committee. Set up in December 1948 by the CoS to produce a review of annual defence expenditure, the committee finally reported in February 1949. Tough on the UK's armed forces as a whole, its harshest proposal was that the Navy should, in future, receive the "smallest individual share of finance".[50] As Hollis stated in his memoirs, "The Navy was [as a consequence] making deep cuts in men, money and equipment. It was quite natural, therefore, that we in the Marines should come under the closest scrutiny".[51]

A corollary of this was that the Navy could not now "afford to retain the Royal Marines Commandos" and therefore they should be "abolished, the Royal Marines disbanded, or retained as a regiment within the Army".[52] Fortunately for the Corps, the Harwood report's findings were deemed "unacceptable" by the Chiefs of Staff, as well as the Minister of Defence, and were duly dropped. Yet this was not before Hollis had succeeded in persuading the Admiralty Board to retain 3 Commando Brigade, but reduce the Corps' overall strength to 10,300 Marines.[53] Paralleling debate in the early 21st century as to the reasons for the existence of the Future Commando Force (FCF), intense discussion as to the Royal Marines' actual and future roles rumbled on throughout 1949 and well into 1950.

Having seen off the Harwood Committee, General Hollis was obliged to handle further scrutiny of the Corps by Whitehall officialdom, this time in the shape of the Long Committee. Established in August 1949, this inter-service committee's terms of reference were, "To review the headquarters and other Combined Operations establishments and to recommend what changes should be made and how reductions in the present cost can best be achieved."[54] Predictably, it recommended reductions in staff and a reorganisation of Combined Operations.

These proposals prompted the First Sea Lord, Lord Fraser of North Cape, to moot the idea of placing COHQ under the command of General Hollis, a plan that was ultimately impractical owing to his existing heavy workload. A further initiative emanating from Fraser was the "vesting of primary responsibility for amphibious warfare with the Royal Marines".[55] It was further proposed that CGRM become amphibious warfare advisor to the CoS.

Yet at a CoS committee meeting in March 1950, the Long Report, as well as Fraser's plans, were rejected by the Service Chiefs. Primarily, it was felt that the Royal Marines did not possess "sufficient experience in the full range of issues to undertake responsibility for combined operations."[56] Consequently, the overall conclusion reached by the CoS was that Combined Operations should remain an independent, inter-service organisation directed by an autonomous chief.[57]

Despite Whitehall's periodic stabs at tampering with the organisational machinery of COHQ/AWHQ, a general consensus as to the Commandos' concept of employment was finally reached in 1949. It was now accepted that the Royal Marines Commandos should specialise in small-scale raiding, for larger-scale amphibious operations would have to be undertaken by the British Army at the brigade or divisional levels, supported by panoply of specialist units.[58] Yet the development of atomic and hydrogen bombs during the late 1940s and early 1950s swiftly invalidated this last operational assumption. As a consequence of this paradigm shift in strategic affairs, the ability to launch full-scale amphibious assaults against a nuclear-tipped "near peer", or "peer" adversary, such as the Soviet Union, ceased to be a credible option.

A year off exploding its own atomic bomb, the UK was heavily reliant upon the United States' nuclear arsenal in the event of war with the Soviet Union, whose own atomic ambitions had been realised in August 1949.[59] In the context of 1951, this meant the UK was obliged to rely solely upon conventional means of striking back at invading Soviet forces. One such way of achieving this end was the launching of amphibious raids against an enemy-controlled coastline, the *sine qua non* of Commando Forces. The key underlying assumption inherent in *The Organisation, Employment and Training of Commandos 1951*, therefore, is that the Royal Marines' specialism in small-scale raiding might very well have had to be resurrected and practised for real in the event of a Soviet invasion of western Europe.

This changed strategic environment was acknowledged by the CoS in March 1951, who agreed a list of tasks suitable for UK amphibious forces. These included, "Raiding operations in Western Europe and the Mediterranean; peacetime training and elementary training in war; the strategic mobility of the Army; the Royal Navy Rhine flotilla; the maintenance of a force over beaches when port facilities are not available; the withdrawal of a force overseas; the emergency discharge of cargoes in the United Kingdom owing to damage to ports"; and "small scale" amphibious assault operations which could include: (i) "the seizure of small strategic objectives in the face of light opposition; (ii) Operations on the seaward flank of the Army; and (iii) Operations in support of the United Nations before the outbreak of general war".[60]

In the context of *The Organisation, Employment and Training of Commandos, 1951*, this list signifies that the CoS recognized (i) that large-scale amphibious landings, such as those undertaken in North Africa, Sicily, Italy and Normandy during the war, were infeasible during the initial phases of a future global conflict; (ii) the potentiality for small raiding forces to play a critical role during the "fluid conditions" following a Soviet invasion of Europe;[61] and (iii) the attendant need for there to be a continued UK defence commitment to small-scale raiding by Commando Forces. Fortuitously, this "changed strategic environment" ensured that the Royal Marines, and not the British Army, achieved primacy in amphibious warfare.[62] In turn, this meant that 3 Commando Brigade could distinguish and separate itself from its Army counterparts thereby guaranteeing, in theory, its "institutional survival".

During Hollis's tenure as the professional head of the Royal Marines, the main responsibilities of his office were to exercise "independent command" of the Corps; be answerable to their lordships of the Admiralty; the discussion of policy matters with the First Sea Lord from whom he received "instructions"; accountability to the Second Sea Lord for personnel matters; and overall responsibility for the administration of the Corps.[63] Inherent in this set of duties was the safeguarding of the Royal Marines' very existence.

A renewed existential threat to the Royal Marines' future culminated in July 1950 when Hollis detected within the Royal Navy and Whitehall a growing perception of the Corps as being "unbalanced and uneconomical", as well as fundamentally "redundant in its present role".[64] Hollis's counter to these hostile views was to recommend the retention of the Commandos and the attachment of "amphibious striking forces to the main fleets", so as to highlight the "unique nature of the Corps".[65] It was against this background of continual anxiety as to the "institutional survival" of the Royal Marines, therefore, that *Amphibious Warfare Handbook No. 10a* was commissioned.

Although Generals Thomas and Hollis, as CAW and CGRM respectively, distilled their own knowledge and expertise regarding the Royal Marines and Combined Operations into *Amphibious Warfare Handbook No. 10a*, it was their individual HQ staffs who were ultimately responsible for producing Commando doctrine and attaining "institutional approval" for this "accepted body of ideas".[66]

As to these individual HQ staffs, the CGRM in 1948 had, by his own admission, a "small composite staff" which operated out of the Admiralty;[67] while during his tenure as CAW, Major-General Jim Moulton possessed a HQ staff comprising a Royal Naval captain as his senior staff officer; a Naval secretary; a Royal Marines colonel; two British Army lieutenant-colonels; an RAF wing commander; and an assortment of junior staff officers supported by personnel from the Women's Royal Naval

Service (WRNS). While Moulton observed that it was a "very mixed staff", truly representative of all three armed services, he nevertheless conceded that it was a "very small staff", and one without much power or influence. This was largely due to the relative indifference of Whitehall and the rest of UK defence to amphibious warfare during this period.[68]

Staff sizes apart, collectively, Thomas, Hollis and their general staff officers represented a "review body" with respect to the conception and formulation of Commando doctrine. Such "review bodies", in the opinion of one academic, "have their own interests to promote, not least of which is a justification of their existence and their budget".[69] As already noted, the last two issues were particularly vexing for the Royal Marines during the late 1940s and early 1950s, and as such would have underpinned the rationale for *The Organisation, Employment and Training of Commandos, 1951.*

Why Was the Handbook Written and For What Audience?

Setting aside fiscal austerity, inter-service politics, ceaseless Whitehall battles to preserve the Corps, and the transformation of COHQ into AWHQ, one of the primary grounds for producing *Amphibious Warfare Handbook No. 10a* was to renew and update existing Combined Operations doctrine pertaining to amphibious warfare and the Commandos.

By 1951, World War II vintage Commando doctrine was, quite understandably, rather stale and therefore in need of revision and re-articulation. Consequently, *The Organisation, Employment and Training of Commandos, 1951,* superseded Combined Operations Pamphlet No. 26, *Commandos in the Field 1945*,[70] published in March of that year, as well as Combined Operations Pamphlet No. 24 (*Cliff Assaults 1945*); No. 27 (*Hardening of Commando Troops for Warfare 1944*); and No. 28 (*Small Scale Amphibious Raids 1945*).

The "influence of formative experiences" on the writing of authoritative doctrine is key. "The challenge to any armed force", according to one authority on military doctrine, "is to distil the continuities from the discontinuities", the "logic" being to "then ... build a new doctrine on the foundation stone of the former, which would inform the doctrine at tactical, operational and strategic levels".[71] This is exactly what transpired with regards the preparation of *The Organisation, Employment and Training of Commandos, 1951*, which drew heavily upon the information contained within Combined Operations pamphlets 24, 26, 27 and 28.

In effect, these pieces of disparate wartime doctrine acted as a collective blueprint for *Amphibious Warfare Handbooks Nos. 10a* and *10b* whose post-war target audience comprised those serving in the Admiralty and War Office; practitioners of amphibious warfare; Royal Marines (Commando and non-Commando trained); and anyone else in His Majesty's Armed Forces expected to operate alongside Commando units. In essence, *The Organisation, Employment and Training of Commandos, 1951* indoctrinated its readership as to what Commandos were, what they did, as well as when, where and how to employ them in the field.

From an institutional standpoint, this requirement to articulate the *raison d'être* of a Commando was of particular importance owing to the fact that in 1951 there existed two types of Royal Marine: the old "Sea Service Marine", who wore the traditional "blue" beret and largely served aboard capital ships; and the "green" beret-wearing, Commando-trained Marine,[72] the Navy's own elite amphibious light-infantryman. Yet as the Corps' authorized history records, "... commando service was not popular with some sea-going Marines and there was some animosity between the wearers of the 'blue' and 'green' berets."[73]

This is perhaps not surprising given the disparity in numbers between the two breeds of Marine, for in 1948 the Corps' total strength stood at 13,000 men of which only 2,200 were Commandos.[74] Regrettably, this antipathy and its accompanying tensions were to persist well into the late 1950s.[75] As one former Marine Commando officer affirmed, "It was to be quite a few years before the Commandos ... were to cease from being regarded as outsiders and accepted in their rightful place as an integral part of the Corps."[76]

National Service

A further factor regarding the Corps' concept of identity and idea of self during this period was the existence of National Servicemen. Setting aside the fact that between 1939 and 1945 the entire adult population of Great Britain had been mobilized for war, in excess of "two million men were conscripted into the British armed forces between the end of the Second World War and November 1960; the last of them [being] demobilized in May 1963."[77] In terms of the number of men "called-up" for post-war National Service, the years 1950 to 1952 marked a peak in conscription.[78]

By 1957, over 300 officers and 9,000 Marines had served in the Corps as National Servicemen.[79] Yet significantly, the Corps possessed "fewer" National Servicemen in "proportion to overall numbers than any other service", the ratio being "30 per cent National Servicemen" to "70 per cent 'long service regulars'".[80] This marked imbalance between volunteers and conscripts owed its origins to a highly selective recruitment process, whereby the Royal Marines deliberately "recruited comparatively few conscripts".

In keeping with The Parachute Regiment, whose own stringent recruitment programme was predicated on enlisting the very highest calibre of conscript, the Corps only admitted National Servicemen who were possessed of a "relatively high level of education", the rationale being that such men would be able to "read maps, operate radios and handle paperwork".[81] Yet, like those Army recruits who had to pass the Paras' arduous "P" Company tests in order to become members of UK Airborne Forces, National Servicemen chosen to join the Marine Commandos had to "complete the Commando course" alongside "All regular recruits and young officers" wishing to qualify for the "coveted Green beret", the exceptions being "the few going to blue-beret postings (ships and landing craft)".[82]

The success of this elitist approach was identified by Major-General Julian Thompson RM, who reflected that the Corps was "fortunate in the quality of its National Servicemen, who were not only given a longer training than elsewhere, but whose standard was higher".[83] While admitting that "without conscription the recruits would not necessarily have wanted to spend time in the armed services", Thompson was nevertheless convinced that "by joining the Royal Marines they opted for the toughest training, and in that respect were volunteers in all but name".[84] Tellingly, "... once in a Commando [unit] it was", in

General Thompson's view, "impossible to distinguish between a National Serviceman and a regular."[85]

Intra-tribal divisions aside, the formulation of *The Organisation, Employment and Training of Commandos, 1951* was designed to help differentiate the Corps from the British Army by highlighting the marked differences between a Royal Marines Commando and his counterpart in an ordinary Line Infantry regiment. While acknowledging that a Commando was obliged to undergo "Sound basic training in normal infantry tactics", so as to be "able to fight as normal infantry",[86] this piece of Commando doctrine placed great emphasis on the "specialist" skills, characteristics and roles of Commando troops.

In particular, it was keen to call attention to its unique "defence leads" in amphibious raiding, sniping, cliff assaults, rock landings, guerrilla warfare, reconnaissance and intelligence work, as well as the capture of coast defence batteries and radar stations.[87] In addition, it stressed the distinctive natures of Stages I and II of "Commando Training", the first of which included the infamous "Commando Tests"[88] that all Royal Marines attending the Commando School had to pass in order to receive the famous "Green Beret".

Under Hollis's predecessor, General Sir Dallas Brooks RM, Marine training had been "modernized" and a "commando course introduced for all recruits and ... for others without previous service in the commandos joining the brigade."[89] These innovations led to the establishment, in the late 1940s, of the Commando School RM situated at Bickleigh barracks, Devon (the modern-day home of 42 Commando), as well as the development of the Reserve Depot at Exton into the Infantry Training Centre, Lympstone, re-titled Commando Training Centre, Lympstone, in August 1970.[90]

Royal Marine recruit training in the early 1950s, as recorded by James D. Ladd, author of *By Sea, By Land*, the authorized history of Royal Marines Commandos, "comprised courses of initial training at Deal, a spell at Lympstone, with field craft and other courses at Plymouth, a period in theory of 38 weeks".[91] Yet as Ladd admits, "owing to the time taken in moving between establishments and for similar administrative reasons, a recruit spent 41 weeks in training before starting his specialist 'Commando 2' course or higher gunnery training."[92]

As stressed in *Amphibious Warfare Handbook No. 10a*, it was the "aim of Commando training that every man should be a specialist of one sort or another and thus be able to make a real contribution to the versatility of the team."[93] Consequently, Stage II of Commando training was designed not only, "To give each man a specialist skill so that all tasks required of a Commando can be efficiently performed", but, "To give further training in initiative, self-reliance and self-control".[94]

As if to further underscore the distinctiveness of a Royal Marines Commando *vis-à-vis* his tri-service contemporaries, *The Organisation, Employment and Training of Commandos, 1951* listed the specialist courses on offer to those who had successfully passed Stage I of training, namely, Heavy Weapons, Assault Engineer, Parachutist (the exception being those serving in The Parachute Regiment and UK Airborne Forces), Cliff Leader, Sniper, Landing Craft Helmsman, Night and Guerrilla specialist and Swimmer Canoeist i.e. a member of the Special Boat Section (SBS).[95] As the majority of Britain's wartime "specialist" units had, by 1946, been disbanded, and there did not yet exist a UK Special Forces (UKSF) community comparable to that operating today, it is self-evident that in 1951 Marine Commandos were uniquely placed to offer the Admiralty and War Office a full-spectrum of specialist skills and capabilities absent elsewhere.

Historical Context

The international and strategic scene in 1951 was characterized by a series of pivotal events centring on a rapidly evolving "Cold War" with the Soviet Union, and the incipient stages of a British retreat from empire. In January 1948 there occurred a communist coup in Czechoslovakia; the British withdrew from Palestine in June 1948; in this year the "Malayan Emergency" against "Communist Terrorists" began; between June 1948 and May 1949, the US and UK successfully executed the famous Berlin Airlift; in April 1949 NATO was formed; the Soviets successful detonated their first atomic bomb in August of that year; in October 1949 the Communist People's Republic was created; and between June 1950 and June 1953, UN forces participated in the Korean war.[96]

Domestically, the UK experienced economic austerity exacerbated by a balance of payments deficit; a convertibility crisis in July 1947; Lend-Lease repayments; the devaluation of the pound sterling in September 1949; and a general strain placed on the national economy by the war in Korea.[97] Notably, in October 1951 Clement Attlee's Labour government, under which the Army Commandos had been disbanded, was defeated in a general election. This seismic political event marked the return of the post-war leader of the opposition, Winston Churchill, who became prime minister for a second time.[98]

Despite the fact that *Amphibious Warfare Handbook No. 10a* was most likely published before the return to office of Britain's wartime leader, a Churchillian influence and spirit nevertheless pervade the pages of this doctrinal publication. These manifest themselves by means of apposite quotations extracted from Churchill's magisterial history of World War II.[99] A quote from Lord Moran, Churchill's personal physician and author of the seminal work, *The Anatomy of Courage*,[100] further underscores the Churchillian philosophy which championed the utility of amphibious and Commando warfare.

By 1951, 3 Commando Brigade RM, the last of four wartime Commando Brigades (the 1st, 2nd and 4th), and the one chosen to carry on the Commando role, comprised three sub-units, namely, 40, 42 and 45 Royal Marine Commandos. In the years preceding the war in Korea, 3 Commando Brigade had deployed to Hong Kong between 1946 and May 1947; and the Mediterranean and Egypt until May 1950.[101] Having reached Singapore in June 1950, 40, 42 and 45 Commandos thereafter conducted anti-terrorist operations in Malaya, operating alongside units from the British Army, as well as in concert with the police and civil administration.

During two years of intense counter-insurgency warfare in the Malayan theatre of operation, 3 Commando Brigade's sub-units killed 171 communists, in addition to capturing 50 "Communist Terrorists". Field Marshal Sir John Harding, the then Chief of the Imperial General Staff (CIGS) remarked that, "It is a record of hard work, devotion to duty and good comradeship of which the Royal Marines have every reason to be proud."[102]

Notably, in August 1950 an additional Commando unit, 41 (Independent) Commando Royal Marines, had been added to the Corps' existing Order-of-Battle (ORBAT). Raised so as to undertake amphibious raiding operations behind North Korean lines,[103] 41 Commando was the only Marine Commando unit to fight in Korea, for despite a request by the First Sea Lord to deploy 3 Commando Brigade to this theatre of war, the CIGS and Chief of the Air Staff (CAS) were adamant that "operations in Malaya were as important as countering Communist expansion in Korea".[104] Consequently, the First Sea Lord's proposal was vetoed.

The respective and contrasting experiences of 3 Commando Brigade in Malaya and 41 Commando in Korea were indicative of the challenges posed by the inter-changeability between their specialist and conventional functions. Moreover, their periodic dislocation from, and eventual reversion to, their original Commando roles assist in the examination of the changing nature of the Concept of Employment (CONEMP) for Commandos from their inception in the summer of 1940 to the publication of *The Organisation, Employment and Training of Commandos, 1951*.

The series of switches to the Commandos' CONEMP over these eleven years should be of particular interest to the present architects of the FCF, for they clearly demonstrate that it is the exigencies of war which ultimately dictate the CONEMP of elite units such as the Royal Marines Commandos, not force design models constructed in peacetime.

Wartime "Special Service" Commandos

The first Army Commando units were raised in the summer of 1940, following the forceful ejection of the British Expeditionary Force (BEF) from continental Europe. Though the brain-child of Lieutenant-Colonel Dudley Clarke, Military Assistant to the CIGS, General Sir John Dill, the Commando concept in fact derived its original inspiration from the Spanish guerrilla fighters of the Peninsular war of 1808–1814, as well as from the Boer Commandos of the second South African war of 1899–1902.[105] Combining amphibiosity with guerrilla warfare, the main objective of Clarke's nascent Commandos was to conduct limited "butcher-and-bolt" operations against targets situated along the coastline of occupied Europe.

Major-General R. H. Dewing, Director of Military Operations (DMO) at the War Office, and Dudley Clarke's departmental superior, set out the original Commando concept in a memorandum dated 13 June 1940. The "main characteristics of a commando in action", according to Dewing, were: (a) "Capable only of operating independently for 24 hours"; (b) "Capable of very wide dispersion and individual action"; and (c) "Not capable of resisting an attack or overcoming a defence of formed bodies of troops, i.e., specialising in tip and run tactics dependent for their success upon speed, ingenuity and dispersion".[106]

Notably, these self-enforced operational parameters are reminiscent of those placed on the Royal Marines in 1924 by Admiral Sir Charles Madden's committee, which, while seeking to determine the scope of its future employment, defined the Corps' duties and roles thus: (i) "The Royal Marines are an integral and essential part of the Royal Navy. They are to provide detachments in war and peace for the larger ships capable of manning their share of the gunnery armaments"; (ii) "They are to provide independent forces to join the Fleet on mobilisation and to carry out operations for the seizure and defence of temporary bases and raids on the enemy's coastline and bases ..."; and (iii) "They will serve as a connecting link between the Navy and the Army, and will supply the Army in war with units for special duties for which Naval experience is necessary".[107]

Yet while Dewing's blueprint granted the Army's "Special Service" Commandos the opportunity of becoming self-contained units capable of executing raids, sabotage, covert intelligence gathering, reconnaissance missions, pre-emptive seizure and diversionary actions behind enemy lines,[108] Admiral Madden's recommendations, on the other hand, acted as a strait-jacket, precluding the Royal Marines Division from its rightful amphibious Commando role, and from participating in much of the fighting during the first three years of the war. Although the first Royal Marine Commando units, 40 and 41, were officially formed in February and October 1942 respectively,[109] it wasn't until early 1943, however, that Admiral Louis Mountbatten, Chief of Combined Operations, warned the Corps that "the RM division must convert its battalions to the Commando role or face total oblivion".[110] Fortunately, Mountbatten's advice was heeded by the Marines, who eventually fielded a further six Royal Marine Commando units.[111]

During the early stages of the war, Combined Operations HQ, the operational tasking centre for Commando Forces, satisfied itself with small "butcher-and-bolt" attacks on the coast of occupied Europe. In the memorable words of Brigadier The Lord Lovat, who commanded No. 4 Commando on the Dieppe raid in August 1942, and was later commander of the 1st Special Service Brigade during the D-Day landings in June 1944, these raids were very much "in and out – smash and grab" affairs.[112]

Officially, Commando raids were defined as being "generally sea-borne operations on a small scale with a limited objective, and are concluded by re-embarkation".[113] Moreover, as one historian has affirmed, "There was no expectation that commando units should engage enemy forces in any substantial number, or should have to overcome enemy defences and hold a position taken in the manner of conventional infantry".[114] Yet as the war progressed, Combined Operations' appetite for bigger and more complex raids grew.[115] These ambitions culminated in the Lofoten Islands and Vaagso raids in early and late 1941, and the raids on St. Nazaire and Dieppe in March and August 1942 respectively. Later that year, however, the course of the war changed favourably for the Allies and with it the desired operational and strategic "ends".

Having successfully executed amphibious landings in North-West Africa during Operation *Torch* in November 1942, the Allies were no longer on the strategic defensive. For the Army and Royal Marines "Special Service" Commandos, this signalled a significant step-change regarding their role and purpose. Yet this alteration to the strategic situation, whereby the Allies were now on the offensive, necessitated the re-roling of Commando units from "specialist" raiding forces to "conventional" ground troops.

Henceforth, Commando units would, due to the exigencies of war, invariably act as "shock troop" formations, stiffening resolve on the battlefield, as well as undertaking hazardous "enabling" tasks beyond the capability of standard infantry regiments of the line. Increasingly, Commando units would be "allocated to theatres of operations not as single units, but in brigades" enabling them to overcome their deficiencies in administration, personnel and firepower.[116]

The dislocation of expectation experienced by the Army and Royal Marines Commandos regarding the intended use of their initial force model stemmed from a variety of reasons. The changing character and course of the war, together with its vicissitudes and exigencies, all conspired against them remaining a niche, specialist raiding force. In particular, the escalation and intensification of hostilities, or what would now be classified as "mission creep", was instrumental in the reconfiguration and re-roling of "Special Service" Commando units into conventional infantry formations.

Unsurprisingly, wartime Commandos were especially vulnerable to "mission creep", for Dewing's 1940 force design stipulated that they were to fight in light order only; be "provided with no more than they could themselves carry and use";[117] and were not to remain on field operations for more than 24 hours.[118] Later extended to a period of 48 hours, Commando operations were, nevertheless, feasible only "as long as the role of the Commandos was strictly confined to raiding",[119] for beyond these means and stipulated time-limits the likelihood of operational success for Commando Forces greatly diminished. This lesson was not lost on the post-war Royal Marines Commandos, whose amphibious warfare doctrine asserted that, "A light amphibious force lacks the punch to sustain a prolonged effort against a defence which has been allowed to harden, and once this has occurred the operation may drag on indefinitely".[120]

Ill-equipped, and lacking, as they did, the requisite manpower and logistics to maintain themselves in the frontline for protracted periods of time, Commando units were invariably obliged to operate under various higher Army commands. Subsequent re-deployments from one ORBAT to the next merely served to dislocate the Commandos still further from their intended purpose and specialist roles, as well as severely curtail their freedom of action. Consequently, leading authorities on the history of the Commandos have repeatedly levelled the serious charge of "misuse" at senior Army officers.[121]

Land Operations

With regards land operations in general, *The Organisation, Employment and Training of Commandos, 1951* was at pains to emphasise not only the potential range of land warfare orientated tasks, but also the flexibility, versatility and adaptability of Royal Marines Commandos in the infantry role: Commandos … may be employed in: (a) "Operations in which the specialised training of commandos is to some extent exploited"; (b) "Operations in which commandos are employed purely as normal infantry"; and (c) "Internal security duties on peace or cold war conditions".[122]

Despite reiterating the wartime accusation of "misuse", specifically that, "If Commandos become deeply committed as infantry they may not be available for commando type operations when the opportunity for them arises",[123] *Amphibious Warfare Handbook No. 10a* nevertheless insisted that, "Although Commandos have distinctive roles and characteristics it is neither to be expected nor desirable that they should be employed in these roles exclusively".[124] Moreover, the Commandant General's amphibious warfare manual for 1951 was unequivocal when it affirmed that,

> It would be too much to expect that commandos should be able to pick and choose the precise degree to which they are committed. What should however be understood is that commandos neither need to be nor thrive if kept in cotton wool; but, if opportunities arise or are foreseen for their employment in their distinctive roles, or roles which approximate to them, then it is commonsense to have commandos available and ready.[125]

Touching upon the issue of when and where to employ Royal Marines, General Sir Dallas Brooks, who was CGRM in 1948, conceded that, "The truth is, of course, that you have to wage war as you can and not necessarily as you would like to".[126] This professional judgement was echoed by Major-General Julian Thompson RM, who counselled that, "the most suitable employment for fighting men is marching towards the sound of the guns, not picking and choosing where they will fight".[127]

This very much mirrors the philosophy of The Parachute Regiment whose famous motto, *Utrinque Paratus*, or "ready for anything", captures succinctly its specific mind-set and approach to warfare. The "warrior–scholar" General Sir Anthony Farrar-Hockley, one-time

Colonel-Commandant of the Paras, was quick to affirm that it was "a regiment for all seasons or it was nothing", adding, "It must take on whatever task it is given and do its best at it."[128] As an elite force with an awesome fighting reputation, The Parachute Regiment simply could not afford the luxury of pre-selecting which tactical or operational tasks it would, or would not, undertake, or the self-indulgence of placing provisos on the scale of its future employment.

Having had their expectations dislocated by the changing character of World War II, the Army and Royal Marines Commandos were acutely conscious from early 1943 onwards that the realities of armed conflict do not conform to such whims. Consequently, the aim of the specialist instruction at the wartime Commando Basic Training Centre, Achnacarry, was "simple and unequivocal", namely "to produce an elite force of high morale, dedicated and prepared to carry out *any* military task asked of it."[129]

While 1951 Commando doctrine admitted that it was "on the one hand uneconomical to employ specially trained troops on non-specialist tasks", it was forced to concede that on the other it was "even more uneconomical to keep such troops in idleness during a battle or campaign".[130] Having fought chiefly as conventional infantrymen from late 1942 onwards, it was therefore somewhat ironic that in the immediate post-war period the "rationale for retaining Commando troops in peacetime" was based, primarily, on the preservation of their specialist Commando skills and capabilities, such as "amphibious warfare, rock and mountain climbing … long range penetration and infiltration", and the ability to provide the "nucleus of an amphibious force in an emergency".[131]

Yet the emerging military realities of the post-1945 world, and the concomitant operational demands placed upon Britain's armed forces, particularly in the area of "imperial policing"/internal security duties, meant that Marine Commandos once more reverted to being conventional infantrymen, backfilling for the Army which simply did not possess the requisite manpower. This in turn, divorced the Marines yet again from their specialist amphibious/Commando role, as well as precluding them from undertaking invaluable amphibious warfare training. Ultimately, this opened them up to the charge of being "expensive conventional soldiers".[132]

41 (Independent) Commando Royal Marines and Korea

As already acknowledged, the participation of 41 Commando in the Korean war of 1950–1953 serves as a valuable historical case-study as to the oscillating nature of the Commandos' CONEMP. It also spotlights, moreover, numerous potential pitfalls for the FCF, for not only does this episode address the dangers of "mission creep", re-roling mid-campaign, deficiencies in "mass", the dislocation of expectation and the critical importance of inter-operability; it also illustrates the hazards of over-specialisation and sub-optimal force configurations.

At the height of the fighting in Korea, *The Organisation, Employment and Training of Commandos, 1951* enumerated seven types of amphibious "raid":

(i) Destruction or damage to bases used by enemy surface raiders, submarines or minelayers
(ii) Attack on vulnerable points on the enemy coastline to divert superior enemy forces to its defence
(iii) Disrupting of enemy communications and supply lines
(iv) Reconnaissance of enemy defences and identification of troops manning them
(v) Destruction or damage to installations of economic importance
(vi) Support of friendly partisans
(vii) Deception cover for a larger operation[133]

By the time these words appeared in print, 41 Commando had been operating as a raiding force since October 1950, and, as such, had already undertaken two of these mission types, namely "attack[s] on vulnerable points on the enemy coastline to divert superior enemy forces to its defence", and the "disruption of enemy communications and supply lines". Later in the war, the unit would conduct a third, specifically the "reconnaissance of enemy defences and identification of troops manning them".

Yet it is significant that the fortunes of 41 Commando with regards amphibious raiding ebbed and flowed during the early phases of the war in Korea due to the fluidity of the frontline. Moreover, the changing character of the fighting in Korea (one that regularly alternated between offence and defence/advance and withdrawal) dislocated the expectations of the Commando unit whose very existence was predicated on a specialist form of warfare i.e. covert infiltration and raiding, as opposed to conventional infantry work. Ultimately, this left 41 Commando incorrectly configured, undermanned and ill-equipped to meet contingencies such as the fierce infantry fighting it was obliged to undertake at the Chosin Reservoir in November 1950.

Never intended to be a "full Commando" but instead a "small unit",[134] 41 Commando had been formed in the UK by Lieutenant-Colonel D. B. Drysdale RM, a wartime staff officer who possessed "considerable experience of raiding".[135] Initially comprising just ten officers and 240 Other Ranks (ORs), the unit had been raised in answer to a personal request by General Douglas MacArthur, Commander-in-Chief of US and UN forces in Korea, that a "British component" join the US raiding organisation "Specialist Activities Group".[136]

Notably, it had been intended that a Special Air Service detachment fulfil this role, but as the British official history of the Korean War records, "post-war" the "regiment had been reduced … to a single Territorial Army unit" and as "volunteers were being mustered, the war seemed to be ending … and the project was abandoned."[137] Again, this episode demonstrates quite clearly the unique qualities of the Royal Marines Commandos in successfully fulfilling a defence requirement i.e. specialist amphibious/land raiding that other units of Britain's armed forces were simply not capable of accomplishing.

At the beginning of October 1950, 41 Commando commenced a programme of raiding and sabotage operations aimed at destroying railway tunnels, bridges, railway lines and culverts on the east coast of Korea, north of Hungnam. Yet within days it was apparent to Colonel Drysdale that the scope for coastal raiding behind enemy lines was "fast diminishing".[138] This was due to a rapid general advance by UN forces towards the Yalu river on the North Korean/Chinese border.

By early November 1950, the US 8th Army was progressing along the west coast beyond the North Korean capital, Pyongyang; in the east, the US 10th Corps was positioned at Hungnam; and the 1st US Marine Division was moving north, traversing the Chosin plateau. Concurrently, the 7th US Infantry Division and South Korean Capitol Division were operating further north still, near the Chinese border. Consequently, the strategically important coastlines of North Korea were in UN hands meaning the "raiding season was temporarily over",[139] and that no further specialist operations were required from 41 Commando.[140]

The danger that the unit would now be unemployed was not lost on Drysdale. Ironically, it had earlier been suggested that the Commando fight alongside the US Marine Corps in a conventional capacity, an option the unit's Commanding Officer (CO) had discounted. Yet the very real possibility of "no action at all" for his Marines compelled Drysdale to decide that the "Commando should revert to training in conventional war skills – as distinct from those of raiding ..." and await further strategic developments.[141]

The amphibious landing of the 1st US Marine Division in northeast Korea at the end of October settled matters for Drysdale who, fearful of missing action, had a signal sent to Major-General O. P. Smith, commander of the 1st US Marine Division, requesting that the Commando join his men. Smith's division, which was "desperately short of trained manpower" and therefore under-strength,[142] incorporated 41 Commando as a "recce" company thereby gaining desperately needed replacements.[143]

It wasn't until 29 November, however, that the Commando joined the 1st Marine Division at Koto-ri. Immediately drawn into conventional infantry fighting, Drysdale's men were obliged to battle their way into the Hagaru-ri perimeter via "Hell Fire Valley" which was held by Chinese forces,[144] who had intervened in the war on 19 October. 41 Commando subsequently fought in the Hagaru-ri perimeter as a mobile reserve covering the withdrawal of Smith's division, and eventually succeeded in fighting its way out, breaking contact with at least four Chinese divisions in the process. On being withdrawn to South Korea in early December, the Commando's strength was down to just 150 men.[145]

Following the Chosin Reservoir action, it was planned to re-attach 41 Commando to 1st US Marine Division, which was now operating as a "normal infantry formation in the line". Yet as Julian Thompson records in his history of the Corps, the issues of re-roling, inter-operability and force configuration were to complicate matters between the two Marine units regarding integration and co-ordination:

... it is hard to see how the lightly equipped Commando could have been used to advantage in a situation akin to First World War trench warfare. A radical reinforcement (to double its strength), re-organization and re-equipping programme would have been necessary to enable it to take its place in the line. Difficulties had been experienced before, and would again, with Commandos organised into troops of sixty all ranks relieving British infantry companies over a hundred, and the rifle troops in 41 Commando were only forty-five strong.[146]

As Thompson points out, in 1951 US rifle companies had a strength of approximately 200 men. Importantly, this major disparity in manpower levels was a decisive factor in ensuring that 41 Commando retained its primary role as a specialist raiding force, despite the fact that its overall strength had been increased to 300 Marines in April 1951.

Having re-equipped and re-trained in Japan during the spring of 1951, in June that year 41 Commando was deployed to the Wonsan harbour area and its surrounding islands so as to "enhance the local raiding capability".[147] Yet as the British official history of Britain's involvement in the Korean War relates, the unit was "grossly misemployed" owing to coalition "politics". US intelligence organisations, operating on the west coast of Korea, treated 41 Commando as a "rival" preventing Colonel Drysdale, and his successor as CO, Lieutenant-Colonel F. N. Grant RM, from engaging in "enterprises without the most detailed scrutiny and control" of their plans.[148] This break-down in inter-allied relations ensured that these "highly trained Royal Marines were restricted to a handful of small reconnaissance and minor raiding tasks" which, although "performed in an exemplary manner and at minimum cost", meant that the unit was "stuck in garrison duty on the Wonsan harbour islands" until December 1951.[149]

Ironically, by the time 41 Commando was disbanded in February 1952, the coastal railway line in northeast Korea was no longer in use, and consequently there were very few suitable raiding targets left for the unit.[150] Yet in 18 months, Drysdale's Marines had executed amphibious landings, cut enemy lines of communication and threatened the enemy's rear areas, all classic Commando operations. Critically, they had also acquitted themselves superbly as conventional infantrymen, engaging in Close Quarter Battle (CQB) with their Chinese and North Korean opponents. This key point is conveniently overlooked by those in the

21st century who champion a future quasi-Special Forces role for the Corps, one that eschews infantry fighting.

Incredibly, despite the salient lessons learned during the Korean conflict, as well as those digested in Malaya, Cyprus and at Suez, it would take the Corps another decade to address the issues of force configuration and inter-operability. A major rethink on these points came about in the wake of the threatened Iraqi invasion of Kuwait in June 1961, a potential conflict which 42 and 45 Commandos, in concert with units of the British Army, succeeded in defusing. As recounted by the Corps' authorized historian, the differences in force configurations were brought into sharp focus: "When Army units took over the Commandos' positions … [they] found [that] the slit trenches of a Troop organisation did not readily suit an infantry company's layout for a defended area."[151]

Even before Korea, this mis-match between Commando units and infantry battalions had been but one in a series of flaws associated with the "Troop" structure on which the organisation of all wartime "Special Service" Commandos had been predicated.[152] As the Chief of Amphibious Warfare's handbook makes clear, in 1951 a Royal Marines Commando unit comprised 641 all ranks, with each Commando possessing a HQ, a HQ Troop, a Support Troop and five fighting troops, each of which contained 3 officers and 68 other ranks.[153] Moreover, the authorized history of the Royal Marines recounts that in 1951 the "size of a Commando was half as big again as World War II Commandos" whose "establishment" stood at 450 all ranks.

Yet even this marked increase in manpower was insufficient, for what was "appropriate" during the period 1940 to 1945 was not fit for purpose in the post-war world,[154] particularly as the "Higher Establishment" of a British Army infantry battalion now comprised 936 all ranks.[155] This major disparity in force ratios was touched upon by Major-General Thompson, who was of the opinion that the old "Rifle troops were fine for raiding, the original task of the early commandos, but being divisible into any two manoeuvre sub-units were tactically unsound in a conventional battle."[156]

The 1962 re-organisation of Commando units therefore sought their expansion in size, "changing", in the words of one former Royal Marine, "from the old troops into a company formation … with the total strength of a 1960s Commando set at 680 men, organised into three rifle companies, each of 109 men, a support company which included a reconnaissance and assault engineer troop, an anti-tank troop as well as heavy weapons troop and a HQ Company."[157] Anticipating these organisational re-adjustments, 41 and 43 Commandos were resurrected in 1960 and 1961 respectively, bringing the total number of RM Commando units to five.[158]

The Relevance of the Handbook to Today's Royal Marines and the FCF Concept

At the time of writing, the Royal Marines are the Royal Navy's own "highly specialised light infantry force of commandos".[159] They are also the UK's sole Very High Readiness (VHR) force designed for rapid deployment around the globe. They are "Joint and expeditionary in nature" and "contribute to the three main roles of maritime power", namely, "Warfighting, maritime security and international engagement". They also contribute to the wider UK defence community by "safe-guarding the UK's nuclear deterrent; protecting the Royal Navy's ships; and continuing to provide the most significant contribution to the UK Special Forces (SF) Group."[160]

Numbering some 6,580 men,[161] the Corps' main operational focal point is 3 Commando Brigade, which presently consists of 40 Commando RM; 42 (Maritime Operations Commando) RM;[162] 43 Commando Fleet Protection Group RM; 45 Commando Group RM; 30 Commando Information Exploitation (IX) Group; 47 Commando (Raiding Group) RM; Commando Logistic Regiment RM, including the Armoured Support Group RM; 24 Commando Engineer Regiment; and 29 Commando Regiment RA.[163]

3 Commando Brigade remains the UK's "dedicated amphibious commando formation" and is a "crucial part of the UK's rapid reaction capability". The deployable high readiness force within the Brigade is the Lead Commando Group (LCG), a "battlegroup of some 1,800 personnel built around a full-strength Commando (a battalion-sized unit of around 700 Royal Marines) with supporting naval, land and air

assets".[164] The LCG is "able to project and protect UK interests at home and overseas by both sea and land."[165] The LCG role is rotated every two years, alternating between the Corps' two remaining "manoeuvre" units, 40 and 45 Commandos, who are on five days' notice to deploy anywhere in the world.

The Future Commando Force (FCF)

Yet since 2017, the Royal Marines have been "undergoing a game-changing transformation programme" by means of the Future Commando Force concept,[166] a project which is predicated on returning the Corps to its old Commando role. As the year 2020 marked the 80th anniversary of the birth and subsequent adoption by the British of the Commando Forces concept, it is perhaps no coincidence that a succession of CGRMs, as well as the Royal Marines Board, decided to evoke the spirit of the wartime Commandos with regards their blue-print for a FCF fit to meet the emerging challenges of the 21st century. In a series of articles in *The Globe & Laurel*, former CGRM Major-General Charlie Stickland RM, and his successor in that post, Major-General Matt Holmes RM, both set out their respective "corporate narratives" for this nascent Commando Force against a backdrop of rapid modernisation across UK defence as a whole.

Major-General Stickland, in his update "Designing for the Future", stated that he had set in-train a "generational change", aimed at producing "5th Generation Commandos", capable of conducting littoral strike missions, operating in the "Grey Zone" of "constant global competition", and able to "deliver early competitive advantage when warfighting with ... Allies".[167] This transformation would, in his view, see the Corps look and operate "less like an Army Brigade" and rather more like a "scalable Commando Force exploiting our commando skills ...".[168]

Yet in order to achieve these desired end-states, the Royal Marines are having to challenge their existing "operating concepts ... structures and ... organisational design".[169] This represents a clear intent on the part of CGRM and the RM Board to physically, morally and doctrinally dislocate 3 Commando Brigade and its sub-units from their collective "norm", namely the tried and tested Brigade force design, comprising three manoeuvre units and their supporting arms, commanded and controlled by HQ 3 Commando Brigade.

In his inaugural message to the Corps in 2019, Major-General Holmes reiterated and rearticulated much of his predecessor's vision, intent and "narrative" concerning the FCF concept. In particular, Holmes emphasised the importance of returning the Royal Marines to their "Commando roots".[170] Citing the operational role of Royal Marines Commandos in the 1950s, which placed a premium on "the roles of raids and sabotage, special tasks as part of a larger amphibious assault, and strategic port or area seizure as the advance force",[171] Holmes focused in on the skill-sets and capabilities sought in a Commando, namely "cross country speed and ability to move silently at night, skill at arms, fieldcraft, small landing craft landings in all weathers, cliff climbing, swimming, endurance and demolition."[172]

It is now common knowledge across the Corps that the FCF will be a less conventional entity, and instead a much more innovative specialist force, adept at operating independently in small teams, or Special Purpose Task Groups (SPTGs) of no more than 200 men. Operating across the spectrum of conflict in Future Operating Environments (FOEs), the SPTGs will undertake deception and "shaping" operations, so as to "enable" the "mass" of others; will facilitate "theatre entry" for larger amphibious forces; and will attack key targets such as C2, logistics hubs and lines of communication. The countering of Anti-Access/Area Denial (A2AD) defensive screens will also be a priority task for FCF sub-units. All of this, it was affirmed, will occur "at reach" in high-risk environments around the globe.

In his most recent "Update" to the Corps, published in the July/ August 2020 edition of *The Globe & Laurel*, Major-General Holmes supplied further key details pertaining to the evolving FCF programme. In the future, Vanguard Strike Companies will be "persistently forward deployed ('forward contingency') in areas of national interest, engaging partners and operating in the 'grey zone' to conduct sub-threshold activity against adversaries, to constrain and present dilemmas."[173]

Moreover, the FCF will reject the old concept of "Littoral Manoeuvre", which entailed "periodic Amphibious Task Group (ATGs) deployments with Commandos from 3 Cdo Bde RM at very high readiness", and instead will embrace the new concept of "globally deployable Littoral Response Groups (LRG) 'North' (High North focus) and 'South' (East of Suez)."[174] Able to "aggregate" (concentrate) so as to "form a larger Littoral Strike Group (LSG)", these "forward deployed" LRGs can, in concert with Royal Naval platforms, Queen Elizabeth-class carriers, the Carrier Strike Group and other force "enablers", form an "Expeditionary Strike Force (ESF) capable of both Carrier and Littoral Strike".[175]

Notably, much of what is currently being proposed is not new. In a lecture delivered to the defence think-tank, The Royal United Services Institution (RUSI) in February 1948, exclusively on the subject of the Royal Marines, the then CGRM, General Brooks, foreshadowed specific themes later raised by the FCF's architects, as well as subjects discussed by Generals Hollis and Thomas in *Amphibious Warfare Handbook No. 10a*.

Aside from addressing the general "principles governing" the "employment; Functions; Characteristics; Organisation and administration" of the Corps and its "Reserves",[176] Brooks chose to specifically focus upon the employment of Commando Forces. In his opinion, "Marine Commandos should be so stationed in peace as to enable them to reach, in the minimum of time, areas in which trouble is likely to arise". Crucially, Army units did not, in Brooks' opinion, have the required "flexibility" to undertake such work,[177] an assumption implicit in the current FCF concept.

Alighting upon the future character of armed conflict, and its corresponding scope for Commando warfare, the CGRM was certain that:

> We shall not be granted a period of time in which to marshal our strength as in the past. All the more reason, it seems to me, to have ready small and highly mobile forces capable of holding the breach at the outset. I doubt that the Army will be in a position to provide forces of this description. They will have too many other grave responsibilities. And so I think that Marines will be called upon as "stop-gap forces" to operate in the early stages until the more heavily-armoured and so slower-starting forces of the Army can get going.[178]

What is more, Brooks foresaw that the next war would be "total" and would be "waged at a tempo far greater than anything the World has ever experienced in the past". Consequently, the CGRM was confident that in any future global conflict there would be a "necessity for the employment of Marine raiding forces." It was envisaged that small groups of Marine Commandos would undertake "minor raids to destroy enemy equipment, to capture prisoners, or to obtain information." Equally, they could be tasked with securing "flanking positions for a major assault", or carrying out a "feint landing". The securing of bases from which "H.M. Ships" could "operate" was another possible mission for Commando Forces.[179]

Again, the parallels between what was expected of Commando Forces in 1948, and what is now being planned for the FCF, are striking. Unsurprisingly, there is a marked tendency in military organisations, which embark upon transformational programmes, to convince themselves that the institutional changes they have conceived are truly new and innovative, when in fact they have merely reinvented the wheel. In his thought-provoking memoir, *Call Sign Chaos*, US Marine Corps General James Mattis reflected that, "History teaches us that there is nothing new under the sun".[180] In relation to the blueprint for the FCF, the existence of General Brooks' farsighted 1948 RUSI lecture, and the professional observations contained therein, go some way in vindicating General Mattis's telling observation.

Technology, it is asserted, will play a key role in enhancing the Future Commando Force's "very latest weapons systems". Consequently, the FCF will have "greater networked lethality driven to the very lowest tactical levels, with tactical precision strike, and will be able to adopt a dispersed, distributed posture: enjoying the virtues of mass (concentration of effect) without the vulnerabilities of physical concentration."[181] Overall, this transformational programme, according to CGRM, will bring about a "pivotal change" in the operational capability of the Royal Marines.

At the time of writing, it is also understood that while 3 Commando Brigade will "undergo a re-organisation to optimise the units to deliver persistently forward deployed Littoral Response Groups", it will continue to retain its one-star deployable HQ. It has also been decided that the Royal Marines will transform into a Tier 2, Special Operations Force (SOF) organisation, capable of operating alongside UKSF and the UK's Security and Intelligence Agencies (SIA), as well as providing Advance Force capability to the USMC and NATO forces in general.[182]

Continuing to operate in extreme and complex environments, such as mountain/arctic, desert, jungle and the urban, the FCF will place a greater emphasis on "Find and strike" and less on "ground holding roles". As the Royal Marines officer responsible for the FCF programme has admitted, the Corps wishes to "get away from a battalion-like model of operating into one that's more dispersed, more survivable in the battle space …".[183]

The abdication of its traditional light and heavy infantry roles, which amounts to precluding itself from relieving Army formations in any future land campaign scenario, is perhaps the most significant proposal contained within the FCF design. Indeed, it is now generally agreed that the Corps has been remiss in pursuing the traditional infantry role at the expense of its own Commando heritage. Given the bitter operational lessons learned during the Afghanistan campaign, this stance is understandable, for successive *Herrick* deployments gave the Royal Marines little scope for waging Commando warfare against the Taliban.

Yet despite assurances that the FCF will possess an "elastic" structure whereby it can "'snap back together' for Commando missions and tasks during warfighting",[184] the question remains: *in extremis*, could small, widely dispersed Commando teams realistically re-form speedily so as to operate effectively as a Commando Group or as part of a larger Brigade force? Furthermore, by abdicating its traditional light infantry role for that of a SOF could the UK's Marine Commandos now be in danger of being committed to various specialist roles which have been devised for tasks which may never be required?[185] In effect, 3 Commando Brigade's sub-units could find themselves either under-employed, or unemployable in a future campaign/conflict that does not require their specialist skills and capabilities, but does necessitate those held by high-quality infantrymen.

"Mass"

Another pressing issue facing today's Royal Marines is the issue of "mass", or more specifically that of manpower levels. The Soviet dictator, Joseph Stalin, was alleged to have declared that, "Quantity has a quality all its own". In the 21st century, it is anticipated that the FCF will be a smaller force whose lack of "mass" will be offset by technology, greater firepower and lethality. Yet "mass" is a key element in the "physical" component of a military organisation's "fighting power". The "physical" component is defined in UK Land Operations doctrine as providing "the means to fight", and comprises "principally manpower, equipment, training, sustainability and resources" and is also referred to as the "combat power of a force".[186]

As is evident, manpower levels and sustainability (a "principle of war" defined as "the ability of a force to maintain the necessary level of combat power for the duration required to achieve its objectives without culmination")[187] are critical to tactical and operational success. Moreover, it is a truism in the history of warfare that a military force never possesses enough personnel, particularly infantrymen, with which to do the job. Regrettably, the Royal Marines Commandos are no exception to this rule.

In August 2011, the Corps' overall manpower level stood at 7,390 men, but by October 2017 (the last occasion on which the MoD publicly avowed force levels for the Royal Marines) this figure had contracted to 6,580 Marines.[188] This statistical revelation coincided with a widely publicised rumour in late 2017 that the Corps was to suffer a cut of 1,000 men, and that it would lose its amphibious shipping, namely the Landing Platform Docks (LPDs), HMSs *Albion* and *Bulwark*.[189] In evidence submitted to the House of Commons Defence Select Committee regarding this existential threat to the Corps, one former Marine stated:

> Lessening the numbers of personnel will only strain the rest. The workload seldom lessens with numbers; it tends to stay the same or seemingly rises. The effect this would have with guys on the ground would be foreboding and create unhappiness within. [A]llowing this would create mistakes in the long run.[190]

Fortunately for the UK's Marine Commandos these defence cuts did not materialise, but what has persisted in vexing the Corps in recent years is an incipient scissor-crisis whereby it has been haemorrhaging manpower while simultaneously endeavouring to sustain a level of defence commitments which appear to grow exponentially. This overload in work has elicited the remark from those currently serving that due to the unprecedented demands now placed on the Royal Marines by UK defence, 3 Commando Brigade is simply "too busy to excel".[191]

Inadvertently, by saying "yes" to every new defence opportunity, units of 3 Commando Brigade had become victims of their own versatility. Presciently, in 1948 General Sir Dallas Brooks RM warned of such a danger. "Versatility", he counselled, "can, of course, be a dangerous characteristic if uncontrolled", because "a versatile man", he reasoned, "can so easily develop into the jack-of-all-trades and master of none."[192]

The validity of this professional uneasiness is supported, in part, by statistics. In 2011, it was officially recorded that 70 per cent of Royal Marines served in "operationally deployable units" within 3 Commando Brigade.[193] Yet by 2018 the number of Marines serving in frontline Commando units had contracted to just 48 per cent.[194] Potentially, this parlous state of affairs has serious ramifications for the FCF in several ways.

Firstly, its portfolio of defence commitments has turned the Royal Marines into an over-diversified and multi-speed organisation. Secondly, in light of the fact that 42 Commando now operates solely as a specialist Maritime Operations unit, 3 Commando Brigade possesses just two "manoeuvre" units, 40 and 45 Commandos, each comprising, in theory, 650 men. This amounts to a grand total of 1300 fighting men. As just 48 per cent of all Royal Marines Commandos currently serve in 3 Commando Brigade, a figure which equates to 3,158 men, this means that a mere 19.8 per cent of the Brigade are deployable frontline combat troops.

Lastly, if the Corps maintains its current defence commitments, then how can those 52 per cent of personnel posted outside the FCF for two or more years possibly maintain the high, intensive levels of specialist training and indoctrination required of a Special Operations Force Marine? The resultant "fade" in skill-sets and professional knowledge would be significant and highly detrimental to the "fighting power" of the FCF, for an elite, specialist force has to train year in, year out so as to excel at the "profession of arms". Conversely, if 3 Commando Brigade markedly reduced its input into UK defence in general, and focused exclusively on SOF operations, then accusations of irrelevance, aloofness and over-specialisation could be levelled at the Corps by its detractors.

A further problem arising from the "mass"/manpower issue is that of battlefield casualties and replacements. Elite military organisations, such as the Royal Marines Commandos who, as a Very High Readiness (VHR) force, expect to be one of the first units to make contact with the enemy, anticipate suffering considerably heavy casualty rates during periods of prolonged fighting. Owing to the Commando ethos, which instils in every Marine "courage", "determination", "unselfishness" and "cheerfulness", the Royal Marines are especially liable to incur high casualty rates, particularly among its leaders.

This emotive subject was addressed by *Amphibious Warfare Handbook No. 10a* which concluded that, "… prolonged intensive action is likely to result in the loss of so many natural leaders and personalities that a unit becomes incapable of special operations".[195] Yet during World War II, the Commando soldier was compelled to "regard himself as expendable, and to accept heavy casualties, as a matter of course."[196]

Despite the existence of the Royal Marine Reserve (RMR), which in times of war or national crisis provides 3 Commando Brigade with "individual augmentees",[197] a scaled-down, highly specialist version of the present Marine Commandos – the FCF – would remain extremely vulnerable to battlefield attrition. As it takes, in peacetime, 32 weeks to produce a fully fit Royal Marine capable of serving in a Commando unit, and 15 months to train a troop commander, the time-lag during hostilities between recruiting and training a prospective Marine Commando, and then finally posting him as a battlefield replacement, would simply be too great. The existence of the FCF, and its concomitant requirement for specialist skills and professional knowledge, which take time to acquire, will only exacerbate matters regarding combat casualties and the necessity to supply fully trained replacements.

The difficulties of supplying adequately trained reservists was addressed by *Amphibious Warfare Handbook No. 10a*, which affirmed:

> Training in the reserve cannot cover adequately everything that is required of a commando marine. The essentials for commando training … comprise basic infantry skills, commando skill, and moral qualities. Basic infantry skill alone could occupy all the time available for reserve training and still be far from complete. Commando skill and moral qualities cannot however be ignored. Not only are they essential to maintain interest and enthusiasm, but unlike much of basic soldiering, they are of slow growth and cannot be covered in an intensive course after mobilisation.[198]

Similarly, "the replacement of casualties in army commandos" during the war "remained", in the view of one historian, "a difficult problem to the end, and they were never as strong in numbers as those who commanded them or who served in them desired."[199]

Defence Leads

Historically, the FCF concept has been but one in a long line of initiatives designed to prevent the disbandment of the Royal Marines, or their absorption into the British Army; to find new roles for the Corps; to remain relevant to UK defence; and to differentiate itself from the British Army. During the last seven decades, these steps have manifested themselves in the continuing specialisation in amphibious warfare; the adoption and maintenance of a cliff and "heliborne" assault capability; a long-standing commitment to mountain and arctic warfare; the provision of RM detachments for Royal Naval ships and shore bases; and rapid reaction forces for the "protection of UK off-shore installations and for counter-terrorist operations in a maritime environment."[200]

Yet in the last 30 years the Corps has experienced several developments and strategic set-backs which have eroded its independence and standing at crucial junctures in world history e.g. the end of the Cold War, and the era of 9/11 and the "war on terrorism". The first blow fell in 1992 when it was decided, in the interests of closer integration with the Royal Navy, to relinquish CGRM's three-star rank. Apart from dislocating the Department of CGRM from the MoD main building, where it had operated since 1 April 1964,[201] this act also involved the combining of the Department of CGRM with HQ Commando Forces and HQ Training and Reserve Forces (HQTRFRM) to form a new HQ Royal Marines, which came into being on 1 April 1993.[202]

More importantly, this fundamental change represented a diminution in the status of CGRM, as well as leading to a watering-down of the Corps' concept of identify and idea of self, for in 2000 the Royal Marines' dedicated HQ was disbanded, the reasons for which have never been fully-disclosed. Tellingly, since 2000 there have been numerous attempts by a succession of Commandants General to define what a Royal Marines Commando is and to codify his ethos. (For a 21st-century definition of a Royal Marines Commando see the Appendix). These stabs at a personal interpretation of a modern day Commando have been of "mixed utility" and inadequately employed.[203] This has resulted ultimately in the absence of a common point of agreement as to what a Royal Marines Commando is and what he does.

As an integral part of the Royal Navy, and therefore not an independent service in its own right, the Corps has suffered a heavy price for this imprecision, for it has struggled to differentiate itself from UK defence in general, and from the British Army in particular.[204] This situation has been compounded by the tri-service/ "joint" culture that has been fervently embraced by UK defence over the last three decades, one that has, from the view-point of the Royal Marines, obscured and diminished their "defence leads".

An excellent example of a diminished defence lead centres on the Mountain & Arctic Warfare Cadre, formed in November 1970 as a non-operational specialist branch, whose purpose was to produce Mountain Leaders (MLs) expert in arctic survival, military skiing, rock climbing and mountaineering.[205] The absence, however, of a wartime role for the Cadre, and the popular perception of its being the "Corps climbing club", prompted Captain Rod Boswell RM, a future OC of the unit, to conceive the idea in 1979 of forming a Brigade Reconnaissance Troop capable of undertaking medium-range reconnaissance and surveillance work.

Configured to fill a capability gap between "local reconnaissance tasks" performed by individual Commando units' recce troops, and the "long range, often strategic, reconnaissance, executed by the SBS and SAS",[206] the Brigade recce concept was endorsed by the then Chief of Staff at HQ Commando Forces, Colonel Julian Thompson RM.[207]

The Cadre's outstanding tactical contributions to overall operational success during the 1982 Falklands campaign (Operation *Corporate*) fully vindicated the Boswell–Thompson initiative, but it took a decade before their concept of a medium-level recce force was officially adopted. In the wake of Operation *Haven*, the 1991 Royal Marines led humanitarian relief effort on the Iraq/Turkish border, in which the Cadre once again distinguished itself,[208] Brigadier Andy Keeling RM, commander of 3 Commando Brigade, directed that the Cadre's designated title should be changed to that of Brigade Patrol Troop (BPT), and with it a major reversal of its primary and secondary roles. From the summer of 1992, the BPT would no longer consider its primary role the training of ML ranks to act as mountain and cold weather instructors for 3 Commando Brigade, but instead "the conduct of medium level reconnaissance in support of Brigade operations."[209]

Brigadier Keeling, a strong advocate of this re-roling, naturally focussed at the time on maximizing the operational and military effectiveness of the BPT, not on the future ramifications of this major exercise in re-branding. Yet while the BPT – now named 30 Commando IX Group RM Surveillance and Reconnaissance Squadron (SRS) – still retains its defence lead in mountain and arctic warfare, serving Marines, conscious of the decline in the Corps' defence profile, lament the loss of the legend "The Mountain & Arctic Warfare Cadre", detecting in this re-designation a palpable loss of prestige and mystique. As one highly experienced Royal Marines officer reflected, "the Cadre was a true name to conjure with and unique across [UK] Defence."[210]

Critically, this loss in status was magnified by protracted operations in Afghanistan. Although the requirement for a "Brigade Reconnaissance Force" was filled by the BPT, this did not prevent Army brigades from utilising 16th Air Assault Brigade's "Pathfinders", 4/73 Sphinx Special Observer Battery, Royal Artillery, or any other Army recce formation that could fulfil the BRF role. At one time, the British Army even contemplated re-roling 21 and 23 SAS Squadrons (Reserve) into a divisional recce concept.[211] Inevitably, these Army-led initiatives stole a march on the Corps whose own defence lead in medium reconnaissance work subsequently declined during the Operation *Herrick* era.

This inability to stand out in an increasingly cluttered market has been exacerbated still further by the BPT becoming an integral part of the SRS. On operations the BPT is deployable alongside other specialised Commando units who form the Brigade Reconnaissance Force.[212] Yet this proliferation of "specialist" recce units has meant that the BPT has been submerged in an alphabet soup of quasi-UKSF acronyms, none of which carry the same prestige as the old M&AW Cadre title.

Consequently, they are of limited utility in promoting the Corps to a wider defence audience.

A further loss of prestige and independence for the Royal Marines occurred in September 1987 with the creation of the Special Forces Directorate. For the first time, both the Special Air Service and Special Boat Service came under the "unified command of the Director of Special Forces", although "Regimental and Administrative Command" of the SBS remained with CGRM.[213] Prior to this, the SBS had been commanded by Headquarters Training Reserves and Special Forces Royal Marines.

Writing in 2000, Julian Thompson admitted that while "This sensible move was not made without some angst on the part of the SBS ... on the whole it has worked out for the best."[214] Operationally-speaking, it did indeed make sense to allow the SBS to be subsumed within the SF Directorate. Yet for the Corps in general this reorganisation was sub-optimal in terms of its defence profile and institutional survival. Tellingly, numerous Royal Marines officers have served as Chiefs of Staff UKSF, but since its inception not a single SBS officer has served as Director of Special Forces, despite the Corps supplying over 40 per cent of all "badged" SF personnel.[215]

A military organisation that has always prided itself on being highly professional, the Royal Marines have had little time for PR agendas, mythmaking, or the petty pursuit of inter-service politics. Rather, the Corps has consistently striven for excellence in every military undertaking it has been tasked with, placing operational success, and the ways and means to achieve that success, at the very forefront of its thinking. Notably, Royal Marines pride themselves in putting the mission first, their comrades second and themselves last. It is hard-wired into their collective DNA to be mission-focused, as well as relentless in the single-minded pursuit of their goals or objectives.

This single-mindedness was to be amply demonstrated by 45 Commando during Operation *Jacana*, umbrella codename for a series of sub-operations (*Ptarmigan*, *Condor*, *Snipe* and *Buzzard*) launched in April 2002 aimed at flushing out Taliban and Al-Qaeda fighters in the mountainous Afghan provinces of Khost and Paktia. This theatre of operations was ideal for 3 Commando Brigade who, throughout the war in Afghanistan, had in place an Amphibious Readiness Group, comprising two companies of Marine Commandos, situated in the Indian Ocean poised to support UKSF units operating in the Afghan mountains. As the UK's premier specialists in mountain and arctic warfare, 3 Commando Brigade was the natural choice for this type of niche operation, moving one senior British defence planner to exclaim that this mission "had Royal Marines written all over it".[216]

During March/April 2002, 45 Commando battlegroup arrived in Afghanistan so as to commence operations against Taliban and Al-Qaeda fighters. Operating at 14,000 feet, 45 Commando carried out company sweeps for insurgents. With each Marine carrying 130 pounds of kit, the unit excelled at this type of hard soldiering, which required high levels of fitness, endurance and determination.[217] Yet despite the limited operational value of Operation *Jacana* (Taliban and Al-Qaeda forces having long departed eastern Afghanistan prior to the arrival in theatre of 45 Commando battlegroup),[218] the fact remains that senior defence planners recognised the specialist skill-sets and capabilities of a Royal Marines' manoeuvre unit, namely 45 Commando, and duly tasked it to accomplish a mission that played to its strengths and professional competencies.

Yet the skilful matching of tactical ends, ways and means that typified Operation *Jacana*, represented something of a high-water mark for the Royal Marines, for successive iterations of Operation *Herrick*, which superseded Operations *Veritas* and *Jacana*, were characterised by a gross misuse of Royal Marines Commando units by military commanders.

Due to 3 Commando Brigade not being deployed to Afghanistan as a formation in its own right, individual Commando units were consequently grafted onto the ORBAT of various Army brigades. This produced several serious problems for the Corps. Firstly, professional frustrations were generated by protracted operations in Afghanistan, where the character of the fighting negated the employment of traditional Commando tactics and skill-sets, which in turn obliged the Royal Marines to fight as normal light infantrymen.

These constraints upon UK Commando Forces were raised by Sergeant Rob Driscoll, who in 2011 served with "J" Company, 42 Commando in

Helmand Province during *Herrick* XIV. In his book *Lethal Shot*, Driscoll recalled that at Commando Training Centre (CTC), Young Officers (YOs) and recruits ("Noddys") were trained to be the "superior force", what Churchill had called "specially trained troops of the hunter class".[219] Yet in the Afghan theatre of operations, the Taliban inverted this assumption: the Marines became the hunted, while the Taliban took on the role of the hunter.[220]

Secondly, a corollary to this is that 3 Commando Brigade's sub-units failed at times to realize their full operational potential owing to the aforementioned constraints. Through no fault of their own, the Royal Marines consequently lost a golden defence opportunity by not standing out from the crowd.[221]

Unfortunately for the Corps, this inability, qualitatively speaking, to distinguish itself from other combat arms has played directly into the hands of its detractors who, in light of successive *Herrick* operations, argue that for all their "specialist" training, the Royal Marines are, at least on operations, no different from ordinary infantry battalions. As has been established, this specious argument has been deployed regularly since the formation of the Royal Marine Commandos in 1942. It is therefore incumbent upon the architects of the FCF to highlight the distinct nature of the Corps and the unique hard capability it can deliver.

To compound matters, since 1993, when the Corps lost its three-star rank, the post of the Commandant General Royal Marines has periodically haemorrhaged further power and influence. This degradation of status reached a nadir in 2019 with the loss of his position as Commander UK Amphibious Forces (COMUKAMPHIBFOR), as well as the operational command of the EU Naval Force (Somalia) conducting anti-piracy operations in the Indian Ocean.[222] In effect, CGRM has been reduced to the role of titular head, or tribal chief, of the Corps, a sub-optimal state of affairs likely to worsen in light of a threat to reduce his rank still further to that of a one-star appointment.[223] If this were to transpire, it would, for example, make bi-lateral relations with USMC three- and four-star generals unequal and, by inference, impracticable.

Requirement for Royal Marine/FCF Doctrine

Remarkably, in the 21st century the Royal Marines do not possess any in-house Commando doctrine of their own, despite the advent of the FCF and an official desire to return the Corps to its "Commando roots". Instead, they are obliged to rely on "Joint doctrine" publications and the Army Knowledge Exchange, "the gateway to the Army's professional knowledge and the principal resource for sharing knowledge, lessons and good practice for doctrine, force development and training."[224] As an online portal, it is "designed to allow effective exploitation of existing knowledge and to increase the intellectual agility of the force in order to succeed on operations."[225]

This is in sharp contrast to the period between the late 1940s and early 1970s when HQ Combined Operations/Amphibious Warfare HQ and the Corps generated their own doctrine to complement that of the British Army's. A prime example of a dedicated piece of Corps doctrine is *The Royal Marines Mountain & Arctic Warfare Handbook 1972*.[226] Drawn-up by Major Roderick F. Tuck RM, GSO 2 (M&AW) Headquarters, Commando Forces, Royal Marines, from December 1969 to January 1972,[227] this 387-page *aide memoiré* was "compiled from the development" of the Corps' "own techniques" in mountain and arctic warfare and "studies of those of other armed forces".[228] Moreover, the "advice offered" in this publication was "designed to meet the special needs of an M and AW Commando group with due regard for its equipment and standard of training and the temperament of officers, NCOs and marines' in the Corps."[229]

Provisionally issued in 1969 to "provide guidance for 45 Commando during exercises in Norway and Scotland in early 1970",[230] *The Royal Marines Mountain & Arctic Warfare Handbook 1972* was later updated by Tuck owing to the "shortcomings of the Provisional Edition", and the anticipated publication in 1971 of the British Army's new training pamphlets on mountain and arctic warfare, which superseded its "Snow and Mountain Warfare pamphlet No 34" first produced in 1945.[231]

In anticipation of these Army-generated doctrinal pamphlets, the Royal Marines decided to pre-empt with their own brand of mountain and arctic warfare handbook that would "act as a complement to them", but would also cover such esoteric subjects as arctic camouflage, concealment and deception, as well as procedures for deep penetration tasks. Major Tuck, one-time Officer Commanding (OC) "Zulu" Company, 45 Commando, was far from reticent, however, when highlighting the limitations of this Army-centric literature, which was "written to cover 'worldwide' Mountain and Arctic theatres for use at Brigade level".[232] "Whilst these pamphlets will be of considerable use in the Royal Marines", he avowed, "as a general guide they may not cover techniques at unit, company and troop level in sufficient detail." "Support sub-units", Tuck ventured, "may also find that they are inadequately catered for."[233]

The overall significance of *The Royal Marines Mountain & Arctic Warfare Handbook 1972*, however, is that it played a key part not only in distinguishing the Corps from the rest of UK defence at this time, but in assisting the Royal Marines in maintaining a conceptual, doctrinal and operational lead over their Army counterparts in the arena of mountain and arctic warfare, a specialism in which 3 Commando Brigade remain the leading exponents.

In the absence of their own distinctive doctrine, the Royal Marines/ FCF may wish to seek inspiration and guidance from the MoD's recent publication, *Integrated Operating Concept 2025*, which specifically mentions 42 (Maritime Operations Commando) Royal Marines and its conduct of operations historically the preserve of UKSF.[234] Albeit only a brief acknowledgement of the Corps' defence lead in maritime security, this recognition is nevertheless significant, for it is argued by those currently serving in the Corps that *Integrated Operating Concept 2025* could well provide the doctrinal basis from which to "hang" the FCF concept, as well as offering a "key lexicon" and "hooks", such as "Protect, Engage, Constrain and Fight" which any future Commando doctrine would have to acknowledge. Instead of vague concepts, visions and aspirations, *Integrated Operating Concept 2025* could be the stimulus for a document that clearly delineates a "Defence required, Secretary of State for Defence endorsed hard capability" deliverable by the Royal Marines.[235]

As already noted, the Royal Marines are currently undergoing significant institutional changes by means of the Future Commando Force programme. As a consequence, they are having to challenge their existing operating concept, structures, doctrine and organisational design, so as to meet the emerging strategic challenges of the 21st century. Against this backdrop of transformation, it is now imperative that the Corps reasserts itself, starts to win the Whitehall battles for funding and resources, and sets out clearly and unambiguously what the Royal Marines stand for, who they are, what they do and what they ultimately contribute to UK defence. This is highly necessary, for in 2021, as it was back in 1948, "most people know of the Corps", but "[f]ew know what they do; far less how they do it."[236]

As part of this process, and in conjunction with *Integrated Operating Concept 2025*, *Amphibious Warfare Handbook No. 10a* should be regarded as a convenient conceptual starting point. As a highly relevant historical document, it should inspire, guide and act as a template for today's Royal Marines Commandos, who urgently require a "5th generation" version of the doctrine Generals Hollis and Thomas laboured to produce for the Corps in 1951. What is more, the historical perspective granted by this piece of post-war Commando doctrine should also serve to remind those currently shaping the FCF concept of General Sir John Hackett's advice, namely, "To see where we are going, we must know where we are, and to know where we are, we must discover how we got here."[237]

Notes

1 Lord Lovat, *March Past: A Memoir By Lord Lovat* (London: Weidenfeld & Nicolson, 1978), pp. 360–361.

2 Charles Messenger, *Commandos: The Definitive History of Commando Operations in the Second World War* (London: William Collins, 2016), p. 424n.

3 Major-General Matt Holmes, "A Message from CGRM", *The Globe & Laurel: The Journal of the Royal Marines*, Volume CXXVII, No.4 (July/August 2019), p. 273.

4 TNA DEFE 2/1770, *Amphibious Warfare Handbook No. 10a: The Organisation, Employment and Training of Commandos, 1951*, Combined Operations Headquarters, Ministry of Defence.

5 TNA DEFE 2/1771, *Amphibious Warfare Handbook No. 10b: Amphibious Raids, 1951,* Combined Operations Headquarters, Ministry of Defence.

6 Notably, Major-General Julian Thompson RM, who joined the Corps in 1952 and is presently the president of the Royal Marines Historical Society, was not aware of the existence of *The Organisation, Employment and Training of Commandos, 1951*. The same applies to two former Commandants-General Royal Marines, Lieutenant-General Sir Henry Beverley RM and Lieutenant-General Sir Rob Fry RM.

7 Harald Høiback, *Understanding Military Doctrine: A Multidisciplinary Approach* (Abingdon, Oxon: Routledge, 2017), p. 5.

8 Ibid., p. 174.

9 Ibid., p. 175.

10 Ibid., p. 27.

11 See Peter Hennessy, *Having It So Good: Britain in the Fifties* (London: Allen Lane, 2006), pp. 158–159.

12 TNA DEFE 2/1770, *Amphibious Warfare Handbook No. 10a*.

13 Harald Høiback, *Understanding Military Doctrine: A Multidisciplinary Approach*, p. 51.

14 Great Britain Army General Staff, *Design For Military Operations: The British Military Doctrine,* Army Code 71451 (London: Her Majesty's Stationery Office, 1989).

15 Harald Høiback, *Understanding Military Doctrine: A Multidisciplinary Approach*, p. 51.

16 *The Fighting Instructions BRd 4487 Vol. 1.0: Maritime Doctrine Primer*, Third Edition, Maritime Warfare Centre, January 2019, p. 3.

17 Harald Høiback, *Understanding Military Doctrine: A Multidisciplinary Approach*, p. 2.
18 Ibid., p. 22.
19 Ibid., p. 142.
20 Richard Holmes (ed.), *The Oxford Companion to Military History* (Oxford: OUP, 2001), p. 262.
21 Theo Farrell, "Chapter 1: Making Sense of Doctrine", in Michael Duffy, Theo Farrell and Geoffrey Sloan (eds.), *Doctrine and Military Effectiveness, Strategic Policy Studies 1* (Exeter: University of Exeter, 1997), p. 2.
22 Ibid.
23 Ibid.
24 Keith Grint and Brad Jackson, "Toward 'Socially Constructive' Social Constructions of Leadership", *Management Communication Quarterly*, Volume 24, Issue 2 (April 2010), p. 353.
25 John Gooch, "Introduction: Military Doctrine and Military History", in *The Origins of Contemporary Doctrine*, Occasional Paper No. 30 (Camberley, Surrey: Strategic and Combat Studies Institute, September 1997), p. 6.
26 Ibid.
27 Land Warfare Development Centre, "Chapter 3: Fighting Power", *Land Operations, Army Field Manual*, Army Doctrine Publication AC 71940, 2017, p. 3–4.
28 TNA DEFE 2/1770, *Amphibious Warfare Handbook No. 10a*, p. iv.
29 See https://discovery.nationalarchives.gov.uk/results/r/1?_q=Amphibious%20 warfare%20handbook. Accessed 16 October 2020.
30 See Bernard Fergusson, *The Watery Maze: The Story of Combined Operations* (London: Collins, 1961).
31 Ian Speller, *The Role of Amphibious Warfare in British Defence Policy, 1945–56* (Basingstoke, Hampshire: Palgrave, 2001), p. 27.
32 Foreword by Vice-Admiral Lord Louis Mountbatten, *Combined Operations: The Official Story of the Commandos* (New York: Macmillan Company, 1943), p. v.
33 Ian Speller, *The Role of Amphibious Warfare in British Defence Policy, 1945–56*, p. 217.
34 See "Combined Operations Headquarters, and Ministry of Defence, Combined Operations Headquarters later Amphibious Warfare Headquarters: Records", https://discovery.nationalarchives.gov.uk/details/r/C5760. Accessed 16 October 2020.
35 Ian Speller, *The Role of Amphibious Warfare in British Defence Policy, 1945–56*, p. 14.
36 Ibid., p. 60.
37 Ibid., p. 97.
38 Ibid., p. 217.
39 Bernard Fergusson, *The Watery Maze: The Story of Combined Operations*, p. 387.
40 TNA ADM 196/65/63, *Admiralty Officers' Service Records (Series III): Royal Marines Officers*, "Statement of Service of Major-General Vivian Davenport Thomas, C.B., C.B.E., Royal Marines".

41 "Obituary of Major General Vivian Davenport Thomas CB CBE", *The Globe & Laurel*, Volume XCIII, Issue No. 4 (July/August, 1984), p. 274.

42 TNA ADM 196/65/63, *Admiralty Officers' Service Records (Series III): Royal Marines Officers*, "Statement of the Service of Vivian Davenport Thomas, C.B., C.B.E., Royal Marines".

43 Ian Jacob, revised by Roger T. Stearn, "Hollis, Sir Leslie Chasmore [Jo] (1897–1963)", *Oxford Dictionary of National Biography* (Oxford: OUP, 2008).

44 Ibid.

45 "The Obituary of General Sir Leslie Hollis", *The Times*, 10 August 1963.

46 General Sir Leslie Hollis, *One Marine's Tale* (London: Andre Deutsch, 1956), p. 161.

47 "The Obituary of General Sir Leslie Hollis", *The Times*, 10 August 1963.

48 General Sir Leslie Hollis, *One Marine's Tale*, p. 15.

49 Major-General Julian Thompson, *The Royal Marines: From Sea Soldiers to a Special Force* (London: Sidgwick & Jackson, 2000), p. 417.

50 Ian Speller, *The Role of Amphibious Warfare in British Defence Policy, 1945–56*, p. 78.

51 General Sir Leslie Hollis, *One Marine's Tale*, pp. 161–162.

52 Ian Speller, *The Role of Amphibious Warfare in British Defence Policy, 1945–56*, p. 79.

53 James D. Ladd, *By Sea, By Land: The Authorised History of the Royal Marines Commandos* (London: Harper Collins, 1998), p. 267.

54 Ian Speller, *The Role of Amphibious Warfare in British Defence Policy, 1945–56*, p. 80.

55 Ibid., p. 81.

56 Ibid., p. 82.

57 Ibid., p. 83.

58 Ibid.

59 General Sir William Jackson, *Britain's Defence Dilemma: An Inside View: Rethinking British Defence Policy in the Post-Imperial Era* (London: B. T. Batsford Ltd, 1990), p. 28.

60 Ian Speller, *The Role of Amphibious Warfare in British Defence Policy, 1945–56*, p. 86.

61 Ibid.

62 Ibid.

63 General Sir Leslie Hollis, *One Marine's Tale*, p. 161.

64 Ian Speller, *The Role of Amphibious Warfare in British Defence Policy, 1945–56*, p. 84.

65 Ibid.

66 J. S. Sauboorah, "The Articulation of War: An Assessment of British Military Doctrine", PhD Thesis, University of Reading, 2009, p. 3, quoted in Geoffrey Sloan, "Military Doctrine, Command Philosophy and the Generation of Fighting Power: Genesis and Theory", *International Affairs*, Volume 88, No. 2 (March 2012), p. 245.

67 General Sir Dallas Brooks RM, "The Royal Marines", *Journal of the Royal United Service Institution*, Volume 93 (11 February 1948), p. 262.

68 James Louis Moulton (oral history), Imperial War Museum, 6 June 1983, Catalogue number 6930, reels 2 & 3.

69 Richard Overy, "Chapter 5: Doctrine Not Dogma: Lessons from the Past", in Michael Duffy, Theo Farrell and Geoffrey Sloan (eds.), *Doctrine and Military Effectiveness, Strategic Policy Studies 1*, pp. 43.

70 *Commandos in the Field 1945*, Combined Operations Pamphlet No. 26, BR640(26) (March 1945), p .3.

71 Geoffrey Sloan, "Military Doctrine, Command Philosophy and the Generation of Fighting Power: Genesis and Theory", p. 252.

72 Robin Neillands, *By Sea and Land: The Royal Marines Commandos: A History, 1942–1982* (London: Weidenfeld & Nicolson, 1987), pp. 134–135.

73 James D. Ladd, *By Sea, By Land: The Authorised History of the Royal Marines Commandos*, p. 265.

74 J. L. Moulton, *The Royal Marines* (Eastney, Southsea: The Royal Marines Museum, 1981), p. 111.

75 Ibid., p. viii.

76 David Young, *Four Five: The Story of 45 Commando Royal Marines, 1943–1971* (London: Leo Cooper Ltd, 1972), pp. 5–6.

77 Richard Vinen, *National Service: A Generation in Uniform, 1945–1963* (London: Penguin Books, 2015), p. xxvi.

78 Ibid., p. 9.

79 James D. Ladd, *By Sea, By Land: The Authorised History of the Royal Marines Commandos*, p. 268.

80 Major-General Julian Thompson, *The Royal Marines: From Sea Soldiers to a Special Force*, pp. 417–418.

81 Richard Vinen, *National Service: A Generation in Uniform, 1945–1963*, p. 251.

82 Major-General Julian Thompson, *The Royal Marines: From Sea Soldiers to a Special Force*, p. 418.

83 Ibid.

84 Ibid.

85 Ibid.

86 TNA DEFE 2/1770, "Chapter 1 – Introduction", *Amphibious Warfare Handbook No. 10a*, p. 1.

87 Ibid., pp. i–iii.

88 Ibid., p. 16.

89 J. L. Moulton, *The Royal Marines*, p. 112.

90 James D. Ladd, *By Sea, By Land: The Authorised History of the Royal Marines Commandos*, p. 482.

91 Ibid., p. 289.

92 Ibid.

93 TNA DEFE 2/1770, "Chapter 7: Part II – Training and Selection", *Amphibious Warfare Handbook No. 10a*, p. 14.

94 TNA DEFE 2/1770, "Chapter 9 – Stage II Commando Training", *Amphibious Warfare Handbook No. 10a*, p. 18.

95 Ibid., pp. 18–20.

96 See General Sir William Jackson, *Britain's Defence Dilemma: An Inside View: Rethinking British Defence Policy in the Post-Imperial Era*, p. 34; Peter Hennessy, *Never Again: Britain, 1945–1951* (London: Vintage, 1993), pp. 461–467.

97 See Peter Hennessy, *Never Again: Britain, 1945–1951*.

98 Martin Gilbert, *Never Despair: Winston S. Churchill, 1945–1965*, Volume VIII (London: Minerva, 1990), p. 653.

99 See Winston S. Churchill, *The Second World War: Volume I: The Gathering Storm* (London: Cassell & Co Ltd, 1948), and Winston S. Churchill, *The Second World War: Volume IV: The Hinge of Fate* (London: Cassell & Co Ltd, 1951).

100 Lord Moran, *The Anatomy of Courage* (London: Constable & Co, 1945).

101 James D. Ladd, *Royal Marine Commando: An Updated History of Britain's Elite Fighting Force* (London: Hamlyn Publishing, 1985), p. 185.

102 J. L. Moulton, *The Royal Marines*, pp. 116–117.

103 Major-General Julian Thompson, *The Royal Marines: From Sea Soldiers to a Special Force*, pp. 445–446.

104 Ibid., p. 446.

105 Dudley Clarke, *Seven Assignments* (London: Jonathan Cape Ltd, 1949), pp. 205–206.

106 Charles Messenger, *Commandos: The Definitive History of Commando Operations in the Second World War*, pp. 28–29.

107 Major-General Julian Thompson, *The Royal Marines: From Sea Soldiers to a Special Force*, pp. 227–228.

108 David Thomas, "The Importance of Commando Operations in Modern Warfare, 1939–1982", *Journal of Contemporary History*, Volume 18, No. 4 (October 1983), p. 689.

109 See Robin Neillands, *By Sea and Land: The Royal Marines Commandos: A History, 1942–1982*, p. 12.

110 Major-General Julian Thompson, *The Royal Marines: From Sea Soldiers to a Special Force*, p. 300.

111 See Charles Messenger, *Commandos: The Definitive History of Commando Operations in the Second World War*, p. 243; J. L. Moulton, *Haste To The Battle: A Marine Commando At War* (London: Cassell & Co Ltd, 1963), p. 202.

112 Lord Lovat, *March Past: A Memoir by Lord Lovat*, p. 268.

113 *Commandos in the Field 1945*, Combined Operations Pamphlet No. 26, BR640(26) (March 1945), p. 5.

114 Stuart Allan, *Commando Country* (Edinburgh: NMS Enterprises Ltd, 2007), p. 90.

115 Robin Neillands, *By Sea and Land: The Royal Marines Commandos: A History, 1942–1982,* p. 15.

116 *Commandos in the Field 1945*, Combined Operations Pamphlet No. 26, BR640(26) (March 1945), p. 4.

117 Hilary St. George Saunders, *The Green Beret: The Story of the Commandos, 1940–1945* (London: Michael Joseph Ltd, 1950), p. 202.

118 James Dunning, *It Had to be Tough: The Origins and Training of the Commandos in World War II* (London: Frontline Books, 2012), p. 4.

119 Hilary St. George Saunders, *The Green Beret: The Story of the Commandos, 1940–1945*, p. 202.

120 TNA DEFE 2/1770, "Part I – Operations", in *Amphibious Warfare Handbook No. 10a*, p. 12.

121 See James Dunning, *When Shall Their Glory Fade? The Stories of the Thirty-Eight Battle Honours of the Army Commandos, 1940–1945* (London: Frontline Books, 2011), p. 184; Robin Neillands, *By Sea and Land: The Royal Marines Commandos: A History, 1942–1982*, p. 49.

122 TNA DEFE 2/1770, "Part I – Operations", in *Amphibious Warfare Handbook No. 10a*, p. 12.

123 Ibid., p. 2.

124 Ibid., p. 1.

125 Ibid., p. 2.

126 General Sir Dallas Brooks RM, "The Royal Marines", p. 260.

127 Major-General Julian Thompson, *The Royal Marines: From Sea Soldiers to a Special Force*, pp. 251–252.

128 Interview with General Sir Anthony Farrar-Hockley, "The Paras", episode 7: "Down to Earth", BBC 1, 1984.

129 James Dunning, *It Had to be Tough: The Origins and Training of the Commandos in World War II*, p. 198.

130 TNA DEFE 2/1770, "Part I – Operations", in *Amphibious Warfare Handbook No. 10a*, p. 2.

131 "Evolution or Revolution – The Royal Marines, 1923–2016", unpublished Naval Historical Branch research paper, p. 3.

132 Ian Speller, *The Role of Amphibious Warfare in British Defence Policy, 1945–56*, p. 13 & p. 84.

133 TNA DEFE 2/1770, "Chapter 3 – Amphibious Raids", in *Amphibious Warfare Handbook No. 10a*, p. 8.

134 Robin Neillands, *By Sea and Land: The Royal Marines Commandos: A History, 1942–1982*, p. 169.

135 James D. Ladd, *Royal Marine Commando: An Updated History of Britain's Elite Fighting Force*, p. 279.

136 General Sir Anthony Farrar-Hockley, *The British Part in the Korean War: Volume I: A Distant Obligation* (London: HMSO, 1990), pp. 326–327.

137 Ibid., p. 326.

138 Ibid., p. 327.

139 Robin Neillands, *By Sea and Land: The Royal Marines Commandos: A History, 1942–1982*, p. 173.

140 James D. Ladd, *Royal Marine Commando: An Updated History of Britain's Elite Fighting Force*, p. 281.

141 General Sir Anthony Farrar-Hockley, *The British Part in the Korean War: Volume I: A Distant Obligation*, p. 327.

142 Ian Speller, *The Role of Amphibious Warfare in British Defence Policy, 1945–56*, p. 119.

143 General Sir Anthony Farrar-Hockley, *The British Part in the Korean War: Volume I: A Distant Obligation*, p. 328.

144 Ibid., p. 337.

145 Ibid., p. 340.

146 Major-General Julian Thompson, *The Royal Marines: From Sea Soldiers to a Special Force*, p. 458.

147 General Sir Anthony Farrar-Hockley, *The British Part in the Korean War: Volume II: An Honourable Discharge* (London: HMSO, 1995), p. 310.

148 Ibid., p. 310.

149 Ibid.

150 Ian Speller, *The Role of Amphibious Warfare in British Defence Policy, 1945–56*, p. 118.

151 James D. Ladd, *By Sea, By Land: The Authorised History of the Royal Marines Commandos*, p. 308.

152 Ibid.

153 TNA DEFE 2/1770, "Part I – Operations", in *Amphibious Warfare Handbook No. 10a*, p. 2.

154 James D. Ladd, *By Sea, By Land: The Authorised History of the Royal Marines Commandos*, p. 309.

155 TNA DEFE 2/1770, "Part I – Operations", in *Amphibious Warfare Handbook No. 10a*, p. 2.

156 Major-General Julian Thompson, *The Royal Marines: From Sea Soldiers to a Special Force*, p. 496.

157 Robin Neillands, *By Sea and Land: The Royal Marines Commandos: A History, 1942–1982*, p. 196.

158 James D. Ladd, *By Sea, By Land: The Authorised History of the Royal Marines Commandos*, p. 309.

159 "Annex A: The Royal Marines", *The Fighting Instructions BRd 4487, Vol. 2.2: Amphibious Warfare*, Maritime Warfare Centre, MoD, 2014, p. A-1.

160 "Annex B: The Royal Marines", *The Fighting Instructions BRd 4487, Vol. 2.2: Amphibious Warfare*, Second Edition, Maritime Warfare Centre, MoD, June 2019, p. 157.

161 *Sunset for the Royal Marines? The Royal Marines and UK Amphibious Capability*, House of Commons Defence Committee, Third Report of Session, 2017–19, HC 622, February 2018, p. 14.

162 42 Commando RM is no longer a "manoeuvre" unit of 650 Marines but a Maritime Operations Commando. Yet with notice, this unit can also revert to a war-fighting role like 40 Cdo RM and 45 Cdo RM. See *Sunset for the Royal*

Marines? The Royal Marines and UK Amphibious Capability, p. 14; and "Annex B: The Royal Marines", *The Fighting Instructions BRd 4487, Vol. 2.2: Amphibious Warfare*, p. 157.

163 See "Annex B: The Royal Marines", *The Fighting Instructions BRd 4487, Vol. 2.2: Amphibious Warfare*, pp. 157–158; and https://www.royalnavy.mod.uk/our-organisation/the-fighting-arms/royal-marines. Accessed 16 October 2020.

164 *Sunset for the Royal Marines? The Royal Marines and UK Amphibious Capability*, p. 13.

165 'Annex A: The Royal Marines', *The Fighting Instructions BRd 4487, Vol. 2.2: Amphibious Warfare*, p. A-1.

166 Colonel Mark Totten RM, "Shaping the UK's Future Amphibious Capability: The Royal Marines' Future Commando Force", https://www.defenceiq.com/events-future-amphibious-force/speakers. Accessed 16 October 2020.

167 Major-General Charlie Stickland, "Update from the Commandant General Royal Marines 'Designing the Future'", *The Globe & Laurel: The Journal of the Royal Marines*, Volume CXXVII, No.3 (May/June 2019), p. 181.

168 Ibid.

169 Ibid.

170 Major-General Matt Holmes, "A Message from CGRM", p. 273.

171 Ibid.

172 Ibid.

173 Major-General Matt Holmes, "Update from Commandant General Royal Marines", p. 253.

174 Ibid.

175 Ibid.

176 General Sir Dallas Brooks RM, "The Royal Marines", p. 259.

177 Ibid., p. 264.

178 Ibid.

179 Ibid.

180 General James Mattis and Bing West, *Call Sign Chaos: Learning to Lead* (New York: Random House, 2019), p. 42.

181 Major-General Matt Holmes, "Update from Commandant General Royal Marines", p. 253.

182 Private information.

183 Colonel Mark Totten RM, "Shaping the UK's Future Amphibious Capability: The Royal Marines' Future Commando Force".

184 Private information.

185 Major-General Julian Thompson, "Thoughts on the Future of the Royal Marines", unpublished paper.

186 Land Warfare Development Centre, "Chapter 3: Fighting Power", *Land Operations*, p. 3–4.

187 Land Warfare Development Centre, "Chapter 1: Nature and Character of War", Annex 1A "Principles of War", *Land Operations*, Army Field Manual, Army Doctrine Publication, AC 71940, 2017, p. 1A-3.

188 *Sunset for the Royal Marines? The Royal Marines and UK Amphibious Capability*, p. 14.

189 Ibid., p. 5.

190 Ibid., p. 14.

191 Private information.

192 General Sir Dallas Brooks RM, "The Royal Marines", p. 262.

193 *The Royal Marines Vision: Think Commando*, October 2011, www.royalnavy. mod.uk/About-the-Royal-Navy/~/media/Files/Navy-PDFs/About-the-Royal-Navy/Royal%20Marines%20Vision.pdf, p. 6. Accessed 16 October 2020.

194 Conversation with a Royal Marines Colour Sergeant, April 2019.

195 TNA DEFE 2/1770, "Chapter 1 – Introduction", in *Amphibious Warfare Handbook No. 10a*, p. 2.

196 Hilary St. George Saunders, *The Green Beret: The Story of the Commandos, 1940–1945*, p. 203.

197 "Annex B: The Royal Marines", *The Fighting Instructions BRd 4487, Vol. 2.2: Amphibious Warfare*, p. 158.

198 TNA DEFE 2/1770, "Chapter 12 – Reserve Training", in *Amphibious Warfare Handbook No. 10a*, p. 24.

199 Hilary St. George Saunders, *The Green Beret: The Story of the Commandos, 1940–1945*, p. 203.

200 Lieutenant-General Sir Steuart Pringle, "Chapter 21: Power Projection and the Role of the Royal Marines", in Geoffrey Till (ed.), *The Future of British Sea Power* (Annapolis, Maryland: Naval Institute Press, 1984), p. 151.

201 James D. Ladd, *By Sea, By Land: The Authorised History of the Royal Marines Commandos*, p. 319.

202 Ibid., p. 423.

203 Conversation with Colonel Ollie Lee OBE RM (retired), 15 May 2020.

204 Ibid.

205 Mark Bentinck, "Chapter 4: The Mountain and Arctic Warfare Cadre", in *Vertical Assault: The Story of the Royal Marines Mountain Leaders' Branch*, Royal Marines Historical Society, Special Publication No. 34 (Chippenham, Wilts: Antony Rowe Ltd, 2008), p. 58.

206 Major-General Julian Thompson, *3 Commando Brigade in the Falklands: No Picnic* (Barnsley, South Yorkshire: Pen & Sword Military, 2007), p. 7.

207 Mark Bentinck, "Chapter 4: The Mountain and Arctic Warfare Cadre", in *Vertical Assault: The Story of the Royal Marines Mountain Leaders' Branch*, p. 68.

208 Ibid., p. 68–69.

209 Mark Bentinck, "Chapter 5: The Brigade Patrol Troop", in *Vertical Assault: The Story of the Royal Marines Mountain Leaders' Branch*, p. 71.

210 Private correspondence with a serving Royal Marines lieutenant-colonel, May 2020.

211 Private information.

212 See https://www.royalnavy.mod.uk/our-organisation/the-fighting-arms/roy-al-marines/commando-brigade/30-commando-information-exploitation-group. Accessed 16 October 2020.

213 James D. Ladd, *By Sea, By Land: The Authorised History of the Royal Marines Commandos*, p. 416.

214 Major-General Julian Thompson, *The Royal Marines: From Sea Soldiers to a Special Force*, p. 583.

215 *The Royal Marines Vision: Think Commando*, p. 3.

216 Theo Farrell, *Unwinnable: Britain's War in Afghanistan, 2001–2014* (London: Bodley Head, 2017), p. 107.

217 Ibid., p. 109.

218 Ibid., p. 113.

219 Winston S. Churchill, *The Second World War, Volume II: Their Finest Hour* (London: Cassell & Co Ltd, 1949), p. 217.

220 Sergeant Rob Driscoll, *Lethal Shot: A Royal Marine Commando in Action* (London: John Blake Publishing, 2019), p. 180.

221 Conversation with Colonel Ollie Lee OBE RM (retired), Commanding Officer of 45 Commando Royal Marines during *Herrick* XIV (2011), 15 May 2020.

222 See "Commandant General Royal Marines Supersession", *The Globe & Laurel: The Journal of the Royal Marines*, Volume CXXVII, No. 4 (July/August 2019), p. 272.

223 Private information.

224 See Army Knowledge Exchange, https://www.army.mod.uk/deployments/army-knowledge-exchange/.

225 Ibid.

226 Major R. F. Tuck RM, *The Royal Marines Mountain & Arctic Warfare Handbook 1972* (Plymouth: HQ Commando Forces, Royal Marines, 1972).

227 Ibid.

228 Foreword by Major-General P. J. F. Whiteley OBE, *The Royal Marines Mountain & Arctic Warfare Handbook 1972*.

229 Ibid.

230 Introduction by Major R. F. Tuck RM, *The Royal Marines Mountain & Arctic Warfare Handbook 1972*.

231 Ibid.

232 Ibid.

233 Ibid.

234 "Part 4: Protect", *Integrated Operating Concept 2025*, Ministry of Defence, May 2020, p. 20.

235 Private conversation with a serving Royal Marines lieutenant-colonel.

236 General Sir Dallas Brooks RM, "The Royal Marines", p. 259.

237 General Sir John Hackett, *The Profession of Arms* (London: Sidgwick & Jackson, 1983), p. 7.

238 I am indebted to Colonel Ollie Lee OBE RM (retired) for his thoughts on the characteristics, mind-set and skills of a Royal Marines Commando.

AMPHIBIOUS WARFARE HANDBOOK No. 10a[1]

THE ORGANISATION, EMPLOYMENT AND TRAINING OF COMMANDOS, 1951

CONTENTS

---

[1] N.B. Although this is a faithful reproduction of the original doctrinal pamphlet, *Amphibious Warfare Handbook No. 10a: The Organisation, Employment and Training of Commandos, 1951,* it does, however, contain an appendix and footnotes supplied by the editor.

Chapter 3—Amphibious Raids

Chapter 4—Tasks Requiring Special Skill as a Part of Larger Operations

Chapter 5—Seizure of Ports and other Strategic or Tactical Areas

Chapter 6—Land Operations

PART II—TRAINING AND SELECTION

Chapter 7—General

Chapter 8—Stage 1 Commando Training

Chapter 9—Stage 2 Commando Training

Chapter 10—Training of Signallers, Clerks, Cooks and Tradesmen

Chapter 11—Advanced Training

Chapter 12—Reserve Training

PART III—THE TECHNIQUE OF DIFFICULT ASSAULT LANDINGS

Chapter 13—General

Chapter 14—Rock Landings

Chapter 15—Cliff Assault

NOTE

Information which may be found in the standard infantry and amphibious manuals is not repeated in this handbook. Such doctrine however must be fully understood by those who are required to adapt it to the special problems of commando warfare.

Landing from 18 foot dories

PART I—OPERATIONS

"There will certainly be many opportunities for minor operations, all of which will depend on surprise landings of lightly equipped, nimble forces accustomed to work like packs of hounds".

WINSTON CHURCHILL.
Minute dated 25-8-40.
The Second World War, Vol. I.

CHAPTER 1—INTRODUCTION

1.   Commando units and formations exist to undertake certain distinctive roles:—[1]

(a)   All forms of amphibious raids.

(b)   Assault tasks requiring special skill in amphibious operations.

(c)   Seizure of ports or similar strategic areas.

They are also able to fight as normal infantry and to undertake internal security duties in peace.

2.   They are therefore trained and organised so that they possess certain characteristics:—

(a)   Sound basic training in normal infantry tactics.

---

[1]   According to the *Oxford English Dictionary* (OED), the word "Commando" originates from the Portuguese term "Commander" or "Command" or "party commanded." Etymologically speaking, the noun "Commando" first appeared in 1791 in George Carter's *A Narrative of the Loss of the Grosvenor East Indiaman: Which Was Unfortunately Wrecked Upon the Coast of Caffraria, Somewhere Between the 27th and 32d Degrees of Southern Latitude, on the 4th of August, 1782.* In 1791, Commando had become a South African term, denoting "An armed and usually mounted party of men, typically civilians, mustered, esp. against indigenous peoples, for forays, reprisals, and the recovery of stolen cattle; an expedition undertaken by such a party." By 1824, it had come to mean "on militia service in the Boer army; engaged in a commando"; and by the time of the South African war of 1899–1902, it was defined as a "unit of the Boer army composed of the militia of an electoral district." Following the creation of the first Army Commando units in June 1940, the OED defined the term thus: "A member of a body of picked men trained originally (in 1940) as shock troops for the repelling of the threatened German invasion of England, later for the carrying out of raids on the continent and elsewhere." See *Oxford English Dictionary*, https://www.oed.com/view/Entry/36974.

(b) Specialised skill and organisation for amphibious operations enabling, them to exploit conditions unsuitable to non-specialised troops.

(c) Ability to operate independently as small parties or even as individuals.

(d) Ability to plan, move and fight fast.

(e) Specialised skill in night operations.

(f) Ability to operate on a low scale of transport, or on occasion without transport.

In addition, units and formations are required to possess a high degree of strategic mobility. They must be able to move easily by sea or air.

3.   These characteristics can only be achieved by units of high morale, whose individual members have undergone a sound basic training, during which men lacking in moral fibre or otherwise unsuitable are retrained or eventually eliminated.

4.   Although commandos have distinctive roles and characteristics it is neither to be expected nor desirable that they should be employed in these roles exclusively. Furthermore, many borderline tasks such as beach landings or penetration on thinly manned fronts, will occur. Non-specialised troops could do these tasks, but commandos could probably do better and more economically. Some factors which may influence the decision whether or not to employ commandos are:—

(a) **Economy**

It is on the one hand uneconomical to employ specially trained troops on non-specialist tasks; and on the other, even more uneconomical to keep such troops in idleness during a battle or campaign.

(b) **Battle Experience and Morale**

The morale of troops kept in idleness while others are fighting will suffer and they will lack battle experience. On the other hand prolonged intensive action is likely to result in the loss of so many natural leaders and personalities that a unit becomes incapable of special operations.

(c) **Availability when required**

    If commandos become deeply committed as infantry they may not be available for commando type operations when the opportunity for them arises.

(d) **Re-inforcements**

    In distant theatres of war, re-inforcements for commandos may be difficult to provide.

(e) **Organisation and Equipment**

    The organisation and equipment of commando units differ from normal infantry and consequently may have to be supplemented for infantry tasks. In particular the commando lacks carriers and anti-tank guns.

5.   It would be too much to expect that commandos should be able to pick and choose the precise degree to which they are committed. What should however be understood is that commandos neither need to be nor thrive if kept in cotton wool; but, if opportunities arise or are foreseen: for their employment in their distinctive roles, or roles, which approximate to them, then it is commonsense to have commandos available and ready.

Outline Organisation. (*See* Diagram 1).

6.   The basic unit is the "commando" comprising 641 all ranks and 81 vehicles at full strength, as compared with 936 all ranks and 128 vehicles in the Higher Establishment of an infantry battalion. A commando is organised as:—

Commando Headquarters
Headquarters Troop
Support Troop   4 Officers and 84 Other Ranks with 4.3in. mortars and 2 MMGs.[2]
Five Fighting Troops   each of 3 Officers and 68 Other Ranks.

    The fighting troops contain officers and other ranks specially trained as landing craft helmsmen, parachutists, cliff assault leaders and guerrilla warfare specialists, in addition to their normal troop duties.

---

[2]   Medium Machine Guns (MMGs).

7.   A Commando Brigade comprises:—
       Brigade Headquarters
       Headquarters Unit   Signal Troop.
                                      Light Aid Detachment.
                                      Defence Section.
                                      Commando Stores Park.
       Three or four commandos.

8.   The present organisation of commandos differs from that of World War II in that all existing commando units are Royal Marines.[3]

---

[3] The first Royal Marine Commando units, Nos. 40 and 41, were raised in February and October 1942 respectively. Following the disbandment of the Army Commandos in 1946, the Commando role was allotted to the Royal Marines.

DIAGRAM 1

COMMANDO ORGANISATION

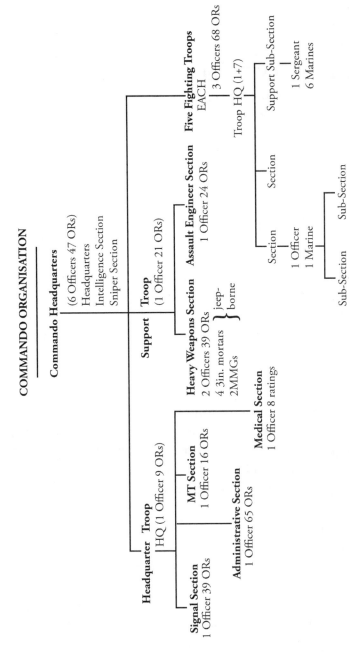

Commando Headquarters

(6 Officers 47 ORs)
Headquarters
Intelligence Section
Sniper Section

Headquarter Troop
HQ (1 Officer 9 ORs)

Signal Section
1 Officer 39 ORs

MT Section
1 Officer 16 ORs

Administrative Section
1 Officer 65 ORs

Medical Section
1 Officer 8 ratings

Support Troop
(1 Officer 21 ORs)

Heavy Weapons Section
2 Officers 39 ORs
4 3in. mortars
2MMGs } jeep-borne

Assault Engineer Section
1 Officer 24 ORs

Five Fighting Troops
EACH
3 Officers 68 ORs
Troop HQ (1+7)

Section
1 Officer
1 Marine

Sub-Section
1 Sergeant
2 Corporals
10 Marines

Sub-Section

Section

Support Sub-Section
1 Sergeant
6 Marines

In addition :—1 Chaplain and 1 Instructor Lieutenant attached.

Note:—For tactical purposes a troop fights as four sub-sections and a support sub-section. Sections are not normally used as tactical sub-units.

CHAPTER 2—COMMANDO AMPHIBIOUS OPERATIONS IN GENERAL

General

9.   Commando Amphibious operations may be of two types:—
- (a)   Normal assault landings by methods similar to those described in the Manual of Amphibious Warfare.
- (b)   Difficult assault landings under conditions of shipping, terrain or weather calling for specialised skill.

In the former type of operation commandos will have an advantage over normal infantry when light scales or transport are imposed, or where time and facilities are lacking to train the infantry in amphibious technique. The latter type require commandos or other specially trained troops.

10.   Difficult assault landings may be made to obtain surprise, to force the enemy to deploy troops on a wide front, to attack objectives which cannot otherwise be reached or to create a diversion. They differ from normal assault landings in one or more of the following aspects:—
- (a)   Landing may be made on difficult coastlines—the most common form being rocky shores and cliffs-or in rough weather.
- (b)   Special or improvised landing craft and carrying ships may be used either to gain some particular advantage such as speed in approach or seaworthiness, or because they are the best that is available.
- (c)   Landings will usually be comparatively weak in numbers and support, relying on surprise and speed rather than on numbers and weight of support.

Naval and Air Situation

11.   The naval and air situation in the area to be attacked will play an extremely important part in planning. In areas in which the enemy has local sea or air superiority, landings may only be practicable from submarine or disguised surface craft. The use of darkness and surprise may make it possible for fast surface craft to drop a small landing force, but withdrawal after the enemy is aware of its presence is likely to be difficult unless the plan can be such that the enemy remains in doubt as to the place or time of withdrawal.

Choice between Seaborne and Airborne Attack

12.   Difficult landing operations have much in common with airborne operations. Ideally, once a target has been chosen the commanders and planners should be free to decide which is the best method of attack. In practice the availability of troops, shipping and aircraft may decide the matter. Other important factors are likely to be the naval and air situation, the practicability of terrain for sea and air landing, withdrawal co-ordination with other operations, and the weather.

13.   For small scale objectives for which airborne troops are not available or which are subsidiary to seaborne commando operations, the parachutists within the commando (see para 101) may be used, but they are likely to require refresher training.[4]

---

[4]   An excellent historical case-study, encapsulating the essence of a successful Combined Operations airborne/amphibious attack, was Operation *Biting*, the Bruneval raid of February 1942. This mission entailed C Company, 2nd Battalion of The Parachute Regiment conducting a surprise night-time parachute assault into occupied France so as to capture and hold the *Luftwaffe* radar station at Bruneval. The objective of *Biting* was to steal a radio set belonging to a Würzburg radar dish sited at Bruneval. This was a key component in the *Luftwaffe's* early warning radar chain, whose job it was to prevent RAF Bomber Command from bombing Western Europe and Germany by means of radar-directed anti-aircraft fire and fighter interception aircraft. This highly successful raid culminated in an amphibious extraction by Royal Navy landing craft.

Surprise and Security

14.   It will be apparent that all landing operations, especially difficult ones, will usually depend for success on the achievement of surprise. The enemy will not be able to keep his defences strong everywhere. In deciding what possible targets to leave lightly defended he will be guided by the importance of the objective to him, and his estimate of the chances of attack. When there is a choice of objectives the ideal will be either to attack targets which although important, are inadequately defended because the enemy does not believe they can be seriously attacked, or to obtain cumulative results from a series of attacks on individually unimportant targets.

15.   Surprise will not however be achieved unless the enemy is kept in ignorance of the attack until the last possible moment and thereafter deceived as to its nature. Security and deception will therefore form an important part of the plan:—

(a)   **Security.** The glamour of unorthodox operations has in the past led unstable characters to talk. Apart from normal security precautions, particular attention should be paid to the security training of planning staffs and of troops who may be undergoing special training and rehearsals. Even those not in the know can often make intelligent guesses with embarassing accuracy. Officers and men must be trained not to talk and those who do not respond to this training must be drafted to other activities.

(b)   **Deception.** However good security may be, the enemy is bound to discover sooner or later that he is being attacked, either by sighting the approaching convoy or at best when the objective is assaulted. When this occurs, the enemy should if possible be misled as to the nature and intention of the attack. Deception may take several forms at different stages of the operation. A cover plan may be required for the embarkation of troops; the course and composition of the convoy may mislead aircraft or submarines which sight it; the assault in a raid may be confused in the enemy's mind with action by partisans or with a larger operation. Deception is inevitably a battle of wits, sometimes over a considerable period. Stereotyped cover or deception plans are nothing more than a dangerous nuisance.

Intelligence

16.   Difficult landing operations to be successful will usually require a detailed knowledge of terrain and enemy dispositions. When time is available, the patient and persistent collection of information should be a preliminary to any such operation. In some circumstances intelligent anticipation may allow information to be collected in advance so that short-lived opportunities for operations can be seized. If this has not been done and adequate intelligence is not available in time, it must be realised that a special assault landing operation will be a gamble and its justification should be carefully deliberated.

17.   The Commando or Commando Brigade has the following sources which may be used to supplement the normal machinery of intelligence:—

(a)   Special boat sections.
(b)   Lie-up parties introduced by parachute or canoe.
(c)   Reconnaissance raids.

Navigation

18.   Difficult landings require accurate navigation to hit off small landing places or limited lengths of coastline under conditions of secrecy. An accuracy of 200 yards is for example required for rock landings. Aids to navigation which may be available are:—

(a)   Markers placed inshore by canoes or further out by submarines.
(b)   Navigational landing craft which should if possible have similar characteristics to the craft used for landing troops.

Radar

19.   Although the last part of the sea approach for a surprise attack will usually be made by night, it will nevertheless be liable to detection

by air search, early warning and gun control radar. The effectiveness of enemy radar coast-watching will vary greatly but will often be a very important factor. Against effective radar, adequate radar counter measures will be required. It may be necessary for the lowering position to be outside gun range, in which case fast and seaworthy landing craft will be required.

Mines

20.   Enemy sea minefields may be another important factor. The time and effort required may make it impossible to sweep in a special landing force. It may be possible however to lower landing craft outside enemy minefields or alternatively to threaten so wide a coastline that the enemy cannot cover it all by minefields.

Difficult Coasts—Rocks, Cliffs and Heavy Seas

21.   Methods of landing on difficult coastlines are fully described in Part III. The ability to make such landings greatly increases the proportion of enemy coastline vulnerable to amphibious attack, and the aim of development must be to increase this proportion still further. The most frequent difficulties are rocks, cliffs and heavy seas.

22.   Rock landings and cliff scaling are part of the normal training of commandos, but for landing on rocky shores landing craft crews require special training unless previously experienced. The technique suffers the following disadvantages:—

(a)   Although the majority of cliffs can be scaled by trained troops, not all are scaleable and full information is required before an operation can be undertaken.

(b)   Vehicles cannot be landed, although heavy infantry weapons and stores can be hoisted up cliffs.

(c)   Cliff assaults are slow if the cliff is of any considerable height, and the troops vulnerable until they reach the top.

23. Heavy seas may vary from rough weather on a comparatively sheltered coast to the surf experienced on ocean coasts exposed to the prevailing wind. Properly trained commando troops and landing craft crews can make landings in a maximum of 10 foot swell on rocks or in about 6 feet of surf on beaches. Amphibians, LCV(P) and LCP(L) with specially trained crews can land on beaches in ocean surf, but this is not part of normal commando training and special arrangements would be necessary before an operation requiring this type of landing.

24. Mud landings are not part of the normal training. Mud coasts usually occur in estuaries.

Landing Ships and Assault Craft

25. The standard infantry lift of LCA or amphibians, hoisted for long range operations in LSI(L)—modified troop transports has been developed to land troops with limited amphibious training on reasonably good beaches. Setting aside the question of availability of shipping, forces of this type are vulnerable to attack and difficult to disguise; the LCA and amphibians are slow and unsuitable for landings away from beaches; and the LCA unsuitable for rough weather.

Alternatives for special assault landings are:—

(a) LSI(M)—converted cross channel packets-hoisting LCA; LCP(L) or raiding craft.
(b) Destroyers, or other light fast ships hoisting raiding craft.
(c) Coastal forces hoisting small raiding craft.
(d) Submarines carrying special craft.
(e) Disguised or improvised vessels.

Examples of typical shipping lifts are given at Appendix A and special landing craft are described at Appendix B.

26. It will be seen from Appendix A that an LSI(M) can only carry landing craft for about 250 men, while she may have accommodation for 400–500. If a commando is landed in two flights the rapid exploitation of the initial surprise may be impossible, especially if the lowering position

has to be outside gun range of the shore. Two possible solutions to this problem are:—

    (a)   To embark only 250 men in an LSI(M).

    (b)   To bring the LSI(M) closer inshore after the first wave has silenced enemy batteries.[5]

Strength of Landing Forces

27.   Forces for difficult landing operations may vary in strength from a few men upwards, but are unlikely to exceed full commando strength. It will not normally be possible to include any armour, artillery other than light artillery such as the 75mm light howitzer or the recoiless gun, or more than a few vehicles. The assaulting force may therefore be almost entirely dependent on what can be carried on the man. Although men can be trained to carry their weapons for a considerable distance, they can only carry sufficient ammunition for an engagement of very limited duration. Ammunition for a limited number of 3 inch mortars and MMGs can also be carried inland by troops, but infantry heavy weapons in numbers, and artillery, cannot be supplied with ammunition at any distance from the landing places. Consequently support from these weapons is limited to their range inland from the landing place.

28.   Even if some transport can be provided, a force making a special assault landing has a, limited punch and must rely for success in applying its strength unexpectedly to disconcert and disrupt the enemy's plans. Its attack cannot be sustained for a long time and the enemy will soon recover from surprise, therefore it must achieve success quickly. The power of a good infantry defence is however still so considerable that even a small force which has captured its objective can probably hold on for some time if the supply of small arms ammunition can be arranged. Special measures will be necessary if tank counter-attack is possible.

---

[5]   Landing Craft Assault (LCA), Landing Ship Infantry (Large) (LSI(L)), Landing Ship Infantry (Medium) (LSI (M)), Landing Craft Vehicle Personnel (LCVP), and Landing Craft Personnel (Large) (LCP(L)).

29.   In view of the difficulty of landing artillery and armour, commando operations are likely to be dependant on naval gunfire and air support to a greater degree than normal. Methods of arranging and calling for support are identical to those used in other amphibious operations, although surprise is likely to be an over-riding factor in deciding whether or not to employ support before H Hour.

Vehicles

30.   The addition of a small number of light vehicles will very greatly extend the range and speed of operation of a special force. At present, and in the foreseeable future, vehicles can only be got ashore on beaches. The following possibilities should therefore be considered:—

   (a)   Landing vehicles in specially constructed light landing craft adapted (or cut) for long range operations.
   (b)   Landing vehicles on small beaches or at fishing or similar harbours which may be
   (c)   lightly defended, and possibly captured from inland by troops landed elsewhere.
   (d)   Use of pack animals.
   (e)   Use of seized enemy or civilian vehicles.
   (f)   For surf, the use of amphibians.

Load on the Man

31.   The shortage of vehicles will make it tempting to increase man-loads. While under some conditions this may be inevitable, it must be realised that a heavy load makes the man a porter and not a fighter. This question must be studied for each operation. There should be no question of the unimaginative piling up of loads because items are customary or might conceivably be required. The aim should be for the man to fight unencumbered, possibly being assisted by porters who become fighters as their load is used up. *See* also Appendix C.[6]

---

[6]   Royal Marines Commandos are renowned for their ability to "yomp" over tough terrain carrying heavy amounts of kit. This is in stark contrast to their "light-scale" Commando forebears whose philosophy was "travel light is right".

Planning

32.   Commando Brigade and Unit Staffs should be trained to plan amphibious assault operations quickly and efficiently. They should have at their fingertips the figures necessary to fit commando units and sub-units into shipping likely to be available in the theatre of war, and if circumstances permit be familiar with enemy methods and dispositions in areas in which operations are likely. For larger operations it may be possible to have organised some forms of standard packet—a unit or sub-unit with its support and control elements which will fit a known type of ship, complete with its landing craft.

CHAPTER 3—AMPHIBIOUS RAIDS

(*See* also Amphibious Warfare Handbook No. 10b)[7]

General Considerations

33.   It is a truism that raids—as indeed any operation of war—should only be made for a worthwhile aim which cannot be achieved more economically by other means.[8] Some examples are:—

   (a)   Destruction or damage to bases used by enemy surface raiders, submarines or minelayers.

   (b)   Attack on vulnerable points on an enemy coastline to divert superior enemy forces to its defence.

   (c)   Disruption of enemy communications and supply lines.

   (d)   Reconnaissance of enemy defences and identification of troops manning them.

   (e)   Destruction or damage to installations of economic importance.

   (f)   Support of friendly partisans.

   (g)   Deception cover for a larger operation.

34.   Higher commanders and staffs may feel some reluctance to accept the effort and risk of committing troops to a raid on an enemy coast. This effort and risk should however be fairly balanced against those of other forms of attack and against the dangers of inaction. For example, a raid made before the enemy has appreciated the danger, may achieve an aim with less total effort and risk than a series of bombardments

---

[7]   TNA DEFE 2/1771, *Amphibious Warfare Handbook 10b: Amphibious Raids, 1951,* Combined Operations Headquarters, Ministry of Defence.

[8]   In 2021, amphibious raids are defined as "operations limited by time, space and resource. They are conducted to destroy or disrupt part of an enemy's infrastructure, to gain information or to create a diversion. They involve temporary occupation of an objective immediately followed by a pre-planned withdrawal."

made against growing resistance. Failure to take an opportunity to deny communications or bases to the enemy even at some risk, may result in heavy casualties and effort later. On the other hand, it would be folly to land troops to destroy targets which can be dealt with by bombardment or to land troops by sea when an airborne raid has better chances of success.

35.   While a successful raid is often an economical and effective means of damaging the enemy or otherwise achieving a required aim, the penalties of failure may be heavy. The difficulty is to assess in advance the chances of success. To give the best chance of success:—

   (a)   The raid should be made at the most opportune moment, which will often be early in a campaign before the enemy has appreciated his danger.
   (b)   The attack should be unexpected in method, time or place, and security must be good.
   (c)   Planning should be realistic; difficulties and dangers should be honestly faced and tasks allotted which can be achieved in the time available.
   (d)   Forces taking part should be well trained and rehearsed, determined, and capable of making the best of a situation which does not develop exactly according to plan.

Methods

36.   Amphibious raids by commandos may be of any strength from one or two men to a full commando or even commando brigade. Raids at brigade scale will however be rare. The technique of special landings will be available as well as the normal technique of beach landings. For small raids, special boat methods are also available.

37.   Raids imply eventual withdrawal. For this reason and to increase the chances of surprise, no more men than essential should be landed. Vehicles may be of considerable help but they will be difficult to withdraw and require a beach both for landing and for withdrawal.

38.   Quick success and rapid withdrawal will usually be a characteristic of raiding, but in undeveloped country against widely dispersed enemy forces, more time may be available. In this case raids will often be more effective if not unduly hurried and a period of guerilla warfare between landing and withdrawal may be developed.

Multiple Raids

39.   A co-ordinated series of raids will sometimes be effective. It may take either of two forms:—

(a)   A sequence of raids designed to achieve cumulative results; for example a series. of attacks to force the enemy to deploy troops in defence.

(b)   A set of simultaneous raids designed to throw the defence into confusion and to achieve all required objectives at one blow.

In the former case considerable ingenuity will be required to avoid a stereotyped repetition of operations against a hardening defence. The aim should be to keep one jump ahead of defensive measures.

Co-ordination with other activities

40.   It may be possible to co-ordinate amphibious raiding with airborne or land raiding, or with other forms of attack such as naval or air bombardment. If the changes can be rung on various methods of attack the difficulties of the defence will be considerably increased.

Control

41.   Experience has shown that all forms of raiding, including operations by the special air service and other agencies, must be co-ordinated at the highest level in the theatre of operations. This co-ordination may indeed be effected at the Headquarters of the Supreme Allied Commander. Detailed planning will be by the commander responsible for carrying out the raid, who may be the commander of a commando brigade, or the commanding officer of a commando unit.

CHAPTER 4—TASKS REQUIRING SPECIAL SKILL AS A PART OF LARGER AMPHIBIOUS OPERATIONS

42.   Assault tasks requiring special skill in larger amphibious operations include:—

(a)   Reconnaissance and diversionary raids (*see* Chapter 3).

(b)   Capture of coast defence batteries and radar stations either in advance of the main landing or simultaneously with it.

(c)   Tasks on difficult parts of the coastline.

(d)   Tasks on low transport scales.

In addition, commandos may be used in the place of normal infantry under the conditions described in Chapter 6.

Capture of Coast Defence Batteries and Radar Stations

43.   Coast defence batteries with radar control can hit the ships of the assault landing forces at distances up to 24,000 yards, or more in the case of the heaviest calibres. Early warning radar can detect them at greater ranges. If the covering, fire plan is required to deal with this threat in addition to covering the assault of the beaches, it has to start much earlier and be more widely distributed. It is difficult to silence guns in emplacements by ships' fire and impossible to guarantee that they will stay silent. Thus at best the intensive fire support required for the moment of the main assault will be dispersed in time and space, and at worst heavy casualties may be sustained among ships and landing craft.

44.   Air bombardment may be successful in silencing coast defence batteries if their number is limited and sufficient density of bombing

can be provided to assure direct hits or very close misses, and is effective against located radar stations. It is however much easier to neutralise defences temporarily than to silence them permanently.

45.   A plan to capture coast defence batteries in advance of the main landing by commandos is attractive, as the physical occupation of a battery is a certain means of ensuring its silence. Difficulties to be overcome are:—

    (a)   The lowering of the landing craft must be out of range, but their run in, if it does not secure complete surprise, will require a covering fire plan of its own.

    (b)   Landing craft can be detected by early warning and gun control radar, although at shorter ranges than ships.

    (c)   Even if the run in and landing are undetected, the assaults on batteries may warn the enemy that an attack is impending, although he may mistake these assaults for the main operation.

46.   These difficulties will be greatly reduced if the enemy radar can be defeated and this is likely to be the crux of the problem. If it can be done, a secret approach and landing followed by an assault, possibly supported by a very short period of intensive fire or bombing, is likely to be successful.

47.   In allotting tasks it will usually be found that a large four gun battery with ordinary local defences will require the main effort of one commando. All troops may not be committed to the initial assault however and one commando may be able to take a second or third battery in succession, but not simultaneously.

48.   Batteries and other coast defence installations will usually be protected by minefields and wire as well as by infantry defences. It is unlikely that the enemy will be able to spare many troops for the latter; but the former will require special measures to get the assaulting troops through.

49.   If the assault on a battery fails, it may still be possible to keep it silent by close range small arms fire. This possibility should be appreciated not only by the assaulting force but by the fire controllers of supporting ships and aircraft, who may be tempted to bombard a battery which has not been reported as captured and succeed only in killing the troops who are keeping it silent.

50.   It will usually be wise to destroy the guns as soon as a battery is captured so that if the enemy counter-attack succeeds, the guns will remain silent.[9]

Tasks on Difficult Parts of the Coastline

51.   The problems and possibilities of landing commandos on difficult coastlines are dealt with in outline in Chapter 2, and in detail in Part III. The possibility of gaining important features by surprise by these methods should not be overlooked. The chief difficulty is likely to be that the main assault on good beaches will be made by daylight; while troops making difficult assault landings usually require to be undetected until they have been ashore long enough to get themselves organised and therefore have to land under cover darkness. If, however, the main landing is made in darkness, it is likely to assist simultaneous landings at difficult places by attracting the enemy's attention to itself.

---

[9]   Two classic examples of Commando raids designed to capture and silence coastal defence batteries (actions which in 1951 would have been at the forefront of minds at HQ Amphibious Warfare) were Operations *Flodden* and *Cauldron*, executed under the umbrella codename *Jubilee*, the Dieppe raid of 19 August 1942. *Flodden* entailed No. 3 Commando neutralising the coastal battery near Berneval ("Goebbels") on the eastern flank, which consisted of three 170mm and four 105mm guns. Operation *Cauldron* required Nos. 4 and 10 Commandos to silence the coastal battery, codenamed "Hess", near Varengeville on the western flank, which comprised six 150mm guns. While No. 3 Commando, for various reasons, were unable to permanently disable the "Goebbels" battery, No. 4 Commando were wholly successful in destroying the one at Varengeville.

Tasks on Low Transport Scales

52.   The demands of infantry and armoured assault forces on ships and landing craft to carry and land their vehicles are very heavy and cannot always be met. The inclusion of units which are capable of operating for a limited period on low transport scales may help to solve this problem, although adequate support must be provided for them.

CHAPTER 5—SEIZURE OF PORTS AND OTHER STRATEGIC OR TACTICAL AREAS

53.   Commandos or commando formations may be employed as light amphibious striking forces to seize and hold:—

(a)   Areas of tactical importance. If in conjunction with a land campaign, this type of operation will in effect be a sea hook.

(b)   Areas of strategic importance whose seizure will form a minor campaign in itself.[10]

In either case the assaulting forces may require the support of other arms and will eventually be relieved by field or garrison forces. These operations resemble raids in the fact that important results may be achieved by bold surprise action, but differ in that the force does not withdraw and must therefore be prepared to withstand counter-attack when the enemy recovers from the initial shock.

54.   The advantages of employing commandos for this type of operation are:—

(a)   Commandos are trained to move and operate on low scales of transport. Their smaller requirement of ships and craft may thus make possible an otherwise logistically impracticable project, or so put forward the date of a project that an early opportunity for carrying it out may be seized.

---

[10]   Memories of 47 Royal Marine Commando's D-Day mission to seize the strategically important harbour facility at Port-en-Bessin, Normandy (Operation *Aubery*), would have been fresh in the minds of those Royal Marines officers who compiled *The Organisation, Employment and Training of Commandos, 1951*. 47 Commando's successful capture of the port on 8 June 1944 was regarded by Sir Robert Bruce Lockhart, Director-General of the Political Warfare Executive (PWE), as "'… the most spectacular of all commando exploits during the actual [Normandy] invasion.'"

(b) Surprise may be gained by landing at places and by methods not considered by the enemy in his defence plans.

55. On the other hand there are certain disadvantages:—
   (a) Demands may be made for supporting and ancillary units normally available within infantry formations.
   (b) Logistic problems may be aggravated by the necessity of relief by a permanent garrison.
   (c) The normal disadvantages of employing specialised troops (see paragraph 4 above).

56. The best chances of success will be obtained by a rapid surprise assault, in which the enemy is taken off his balance and is given no chance to regain it. A light amphibious force lacks the punch to sustain a prolonged effort against a defence which has been allowed to harden, and once this has occurred the operation may drag on indefinitely.

57. When a strategic objective has been taken, the force is likely to be faced with a host of administrative and civil problems. Although military administration officers may be available, many problems are likely to be referred to the force commander and absorb a great deal of his time. It may be desirable to appoint a deputy to deal with these problems so that the commander is kept free to deal with the problems of mopping-up and organising defence against counter-attack.

58. An amphibious force operating on light scales may be able to take with it only what is essential for the assault and immediate consolidation. Arrangements must be made for what has been left behind to join up with it. This will comprise:—
   (a) Personnel and vehicles cut out by severely limited loading tables.
   (b) For strategic objectives, the fighting and administrative units of all three Services required to consolidate the defence.
   Someone of sufficient standing to represent the force commander with planning and movement staffs should be left in charge of arrangements for bringing these forward.

CHAPTER 6—LAND OPERATIONS

59.　Commandos in purely land operations may be employed in:—
- (a)　Operations in which the specialised training of commandos is to some extent exploited.
- (b)　Operations in which commandos are employed purely as normal infantry.
- (c)　Internal security duties on peace or cold war conditions.

60.　Operations in which the special characteristics of commandos are exploited are generally speaking those for which an infantry battalion would require specialised training and some degree of re-organisation.

Employment in Place of Infantry

61.　If commandos are employed as normal infantry, consideration should be given to the following problems which are likely to arise:—
- (a)　**Organisation.** The commando is organised in five troops as opposed to the infantry battalion's four rifle companies. This, coupled with the fact that the Commando has fewer men and supporting weapons and no carriers or anti-tank guns, will necessitate certain adjustments.
- (b)　**Support.** A commando brigade will require the same allocation of artillery and other supporting arms as that required by infantry employed in similar roles. The commando having no anti-tank platoon will require an additional allocation of anti-tank weapons.

(c) **Re-inforcements.** The provision of trained personnel as re-inforcements is likely to be difficult if heavy casualties occur in distant theatres of war. Recovered wounded must be returned to their own commando and not absorbed into the general infantry pool.

Subject to these factors and to the considerations described in Chapter 1, commandos are able to take their place as infantry in battle.

Internal Security Duties in Peace

62.　The high value placed on individual skill and self-reliance makes commandos of considerable value in internal security duties in peace or cold war conditions.

63.　The comparative strategic mobility, gained by the light scale of transport and administrative stores of commandos, adds to this value by enabling them to be moved quickly to centres of trouble. The strategic mobility gained by light transport scales should not be forfeited by allowing commandos to become anchored either by garrison duties or by accumulated stores.

PART II—TRAINING AND SELECTION

"… a man of character in peace becomes a man of courage in war".

LORD MORAN.

The Anatomy of Courage.

CHAPTER 7—GENERAL

64.   The duties of commandos described in Part I require that officers and men in commandos should be trained and selected to possess certain characteristics:—

    (a)   High morale, alertness, intelligence, self-reliance and physical fitness.

    (b)   Skill as infantry soldiers with the addition of skill in commando operations.

    (c)   Specialist skill in particular duties within the commando.

Morale and Commando Spirit

65.   The man of character in peace is the man of courage in war. Character building is therefore a vital part of training. At every stage of commando training particular attention must be paid to:—

    Determination.

    Intelligence and alertness.

    Individual initiative and self-reliance.

    Enthusiasm and cheerfulness under difficulties.

    Comradeship.

    Although rigorous training is important in producing hardiness and self-confidence, the spirit in which it is taken is vital. A man of only moderate physique with a high spirit will do better in war than a mass of muscle who lacks the spark. Nevertheless a man with a definite physical handicap should be eliminated or he may become a drag on his comrades.[11]

---

[11]   In 2021, the "Commando Spirit" comprises "Unselfishness, Cheerfulness in adversity, Courage, and Determination".

Skill

66.   Infantry tactics are teamwork. Each man must be trained to take his place in the team by:—

(a)   A high personal standard of marksmanship, weapon handling and fieldcraft.

(b)   Knowing what is required of him tactically and using his own resource and initiative to achieve it.

67.   First the commando soldier must be a highly skilled infantryman but secondly he must be an expert in his own branch of infantry work. He must:—

(a)   Be able to move fast across any country and be independent of roads.

(b)   Be very happy to fight at night.

(c)   Be ready and able to fight in small parties or on his own.

(d)   Be able to land on coast impracticable to normal infantry and to follow climbing leaders in cliff assault.

Specialists

68.   Specialists are of two kinds:—

(a)   Full time specialists—assault engineers, heavy weapons detachments, signallers, etc.

(b)   Alternative specialists—parachutists, climbing leaders, etc. (*See* Chapter 9, para. 96 (*b*).).

It is the aim of commando training that every man should be a specialist of one sort or another and thus be able to make a real contribution to the versatility of the team.

Selection

69.   There are some men who will never make commando. soldiers and there are some who only require the very minimum of training to become exceptionally good ones. Between these two extremes lies the majority of men. The system of training should not wastefully discard

men who can be trained, nor should it send into commandos poor spirited or stupid men, or those handicapped physically.

70.   Regulars enlisted in peace time are all volunteers for the service of their choice. Marines who cannot become fit for commandos are discharged from the service either "Unsuitable" or "Physically Unfit", although exception to this rule may be made for men with minor physical disabilities which do not prevent them carrying out specialist duties. It is therefore necessary to make a real effort to re-train a man before getting rid of him. Nevertheless, men seriously lacking in character and determination are no asset to the service but are a constant source of trouble and expense. It is therefore best, once a man is established as genuinely untrainable, to discharge him. Special arrangements may be necessary for national service men who are required to serve their full time, but unsuitable men should not go to commandos.

71.   In war when the services are largely conscript a high rate of rejection from commandos, may be acceptable. Two points are likely to be important:—

(a)   Men should not be rejected during training on trivial grounds but a genuine effort should be made to bring men up to the standard required.

(b)   Commanding Officers of field units should have power in the last resort to reject officers and men. If these officers and men are given a second chance in commandos, it must be with the knowledge of their new Commanding Officers.

72.   Ranks rejected from commandos will be returned to training (RTT). At the Commando School, the Commandant will examine cases individually and decide what re-training is necessary. When he becomes convinced that a man cannot be re-trained for commando service, he will ask for disposal instructions, making any necessary recommendation for future employment. The term "Returned to Unit" (RTU), inferring as it does a reflection on non–commando units, should not be employed.

Volunteering

73.   A man who has no ideas on where and how he wants to serve is apathetic, and apathy is the arch-enemy of character. It encourages morale and initiative if men can have some say in their future. Furthermore, a man who volunteers for front line service has gone some way towards showing that he has the spirit necessary for it. Men should therefore be encouraged to volunteer for commando or other service, even though it is unlikely that everyone's wish can be granted.

74.   In peacetime marines completing recruit training are allowed to state their preference for service as between H.M. Ships and Commandos. Efforts are made to ensure that some men in each squad go each way and that the best men get their choice. During their service, regulars are likely to be required to serve at some time both at sea and in commandos, but a proportion of senior NCOs and older corporals and marines will be allowed to specialise completely.[12]

75.   In wartime, commandos will as far as possible be found from volunteers, and efforts will be made gradually to change over men who wish it between ship and commando service. In accepting volunteers it is important to guard against:—
   (a)   The man with a bad record who volunteers—sometimes involuntarily—for the purpose of getting out of his unit.
   (b)   The man who is attracted by glamour and volunteers without the character or nerve necessary for commando service.

Preliminary Training

76.   Commando training as described in this handbook starts after the completion of basic infantry training. A man must be disciplined and skilled in weapons and field craft before commencing it. He should be physically fit and have made progress in his physical build-up which will be complete during commando training. It will be a great advantage if he can swim and is confident in water.

---
[12]   Non-Commissioned Officers (NCOs).

Commando Training

77.   Commando training comprises two stages:—

Stage I—Six Weeks.   A basic course designed to fit a man to take his place in a fighting troop.

Stage II—Six to eight Weeks.   A series of alternative courses designed either to fit a man to take his place in certain specialist duties, or to qualify him as an alternative specialist.

Stage II as well as Stage I is designed to build up character and initiative.

78.   In peacetime, Commando II training of Royal Marines is arranged so that about half the men undergoing it can qualify for paid specialist qualifications (3rd class in the case of Marines). These men do a slightly longer course than the remainder.

79.   A man can be drafted after Stage I training, but a Commando cannot remain efficient if all or a large proportion of men are so drafted. If possible every man except those described in Chapter 10 should do both stages.

80.   Under war conditions Stage I training has sometimes been reduced to three weeks for. trained men, but less than four weeks is never very satisfactory.

National Service Men

81.   National Service men will do a shorter preliminary training than regulars but non Specialists will do the full Stage I Commando Course. They will not normally do Stage II training.

CHAPTER 8—STAGE I COMMANDO TRAINING

General

82.　Stage I Commando Training covers the essentials required by every man in a commando, and more especially by every man in a fighting troop. It comprises:—

- (*a*)　Commando spirit and skills.
- (*b*)　Infantry tactics—from bren and rifle group to platoon or troop.
- (*c*)　Night training.
- (*d*)　Amphibious training.
- (*e*)　Parades, inspections and marches.

Risk

83.　Rigorous and realistic training can be done without undue risk of accidents. Some risk may be necessary but a high accident rate due to carelessness and ill-discipline should never be accepted.

Commando Spirit and Skills

84.　Bearing in mind that feats of physique and nerve, although of value in themselves are chiefly important for the spirit in which they are taken, men are progressively training throughout the course to pass a series of commando tests which may vary, in detail but should include:—

- (*a*)　**Rope and Balance Work.** Movement on ropes and balance walks at heights up to 20 feet-nerve and personal determination.

(b) **Speed Marching.** 9 miles in 90 minutes without straggling or loss of step—teamwork, determination and discipline under stress.

(c) **Speed Scramble.** Movement in very rough country at high speeds—determination and self-discipline within a small team.

(d) **Cross Country.** About 30 miles in moor or mountain country, trainees on their own in small teams marching by map and compass taking the weather as it comes—self reliance, self-discipline within small teams and map reading.[13]

85.   In the early part of the course, correct methods of scrambling, cross-country marching and load carrying should be taught. These are described in MTP 90—Manual of Snow and Mountain Warfare Part III, Appendix E. Map and compass work must be taught so that small teams without officers or NCOs can navigate themselves on the cross-country test. The elements of living out should also be explained.

86.   With the exception of the speed march, men should work in small teams as far as possible of the same rank, so that teams of marines can keep themselves going without the constant presence of officers and NCOs. Instructors must however check performance so that slack work does not get by.

87.   A team which does its training doggedly while hating every minute of it, gets some value out of it. To get full value however, teams must be taught to tackle the work with enthusiasm and to get satisfaction from

---

[13]   In 2021, the Commando Tests comprise: a six-mile "Endurance" course (carrying full fighting order: 21Ibs and a 9Ib rifle) which must be completed in 73 minutes by recruits and 71 minutes by Young Officers (YOs); a nine-mile "speed" march (carrying full fighting order: 21lbs and a 9lb rifle), to be completed in 90 minutes by recruits and YOs. This is followed by a marksmanship test, where the recruit must hit 6 out of 10 shots at a 25m target; a Tarzan Assault course (carrying full fighting order: 21lbs and a 9lb rifle), to be completed in 13 minutes by recruits and 12 minutes by YOs; and a 30-mile speed march (carrying 40lbs of kit and a 9lb rifle), to be completed in 8 hours by recruits and 7 hours by YOs. On the successful completion of all four tests, trainee recruits and YOs receive their Green Beret.

mastering conditions which would otherwise master them. They must finish with their tails up.

Infantry Tactics

88.   Standard infantry tactics should be taught and confirmed by field firing, which should include battle innoculation.

89.   Emphasis throughout must be placed on each man understanding what the sub-unit is doing and being able to take an aggressive and intelligent part in the battle, if necessary without specific orders.

Night Training

90.   The object of night training is to teach men to regard the darkness as a friend and ally and to be confident that they can operate even more successfully at night than by day. Training should be thorough and progressive throughout the course. Its earlier stages should be co-ordinated with cross-country and scrambling and its later combined with patrolling, rock landings and cliff assault. Night shooting should be taught as part of weapon training in preliminary training.

91.   The ability to be silent and to keep still should be practiced by day as well as night. Many men have a habit of noisy and careless talk and movement which they must overcome. Each man must know how to do his job at night without continual orders, and be sufficiently confident not to want to bunch or talk.

Amphibious Training

92.   Amphibious training should be based on rock landings and cliff assault. Men should reach the standard of jumping ashore confidently from a boat kedged off rocks in a six foot swell, and roping up and down without delay, by day and night. This type of training forms a progressive stage from the early training in ropework and scrambling.

Parades, Inspections and Marches

93.   Men start the course knowing how to drill on parade under fair conditions. They must learn to take a pride in keeping high standards under bad conditions. This will be achieved by:—

(a) Rigorous inspections and a short spell of drill on morning parades.

(b) Insistence on first class standards at all casual parades and marches.

(c) Under sensible and sympathetic leadership, insistence that men get a grip on themselves and march and drill properly when conditions are bad and they are exhausted.

Example and leadership play a paramount part in this important training, the value of which lies in teaching men that self-control must be retained in all circumstances.

Singing

94.   Singing on the march should be taught and encouraged. It should be the pride of an instructor to bring his class home singing on a wet night after a hard day's training.

CHAPTER 9—STAGE II COMMANDO TRAINING

General

95.   The objects of Stage II Commando Training are:—

    (a)   To give each man a specialist skill so that all tasks required of a Commando can be efficiently performed.

    (b)   To give further training in initiative, self-reliance and self. control.

96.   The fully trained Commando has a high proportion of officers and men in the Fighting Troops who are, in addition to their normal training, trained as specialists in an alternative role. Unlike full time specialists these men fight as members of Fighting Troops unless required to carry out their specialist role in a particular operation.

    Stage II Commando Training comprises the following courses:—

    (a) **Full-time Specialists**

            Heavy Weapons—MMG and 3 inch Mortar

            Assault Engineer

    (b) **Alternative Specialists**

            Parachutist

            Cliff Leader

            Sniper

            Landing Craft Helmsman

            Night and Guerilla Specialist

            Swimmer Canoeist

    These courses are alternatives, but there is no objection to an occasional man training for his second tour of service in commandos taking up a suitable second specialist, line. In the case of parachutists, it will be necessary for some men to do this, so that a complete parachute detachment can be formed when required.

97.   Some officers and NCOs should do second stage training of each type. It is however more important for officers to do platoon and company commanders courses at the School of Infantry and for NCOs to qualify for promotion at the NCOs School. Consequently the number of officers and NCOs doing Stage II training is likely to be limited. To some extent this will be offset by the presence among the officers and NCOs of a commando and those with instructional experience.

98.   In selecting ranks for Stage II courses, attention should as far as practicable, within the requirements of the service, be paid to individual inclination and aptitudes.

Heavy Weapons

99.   Ranks drafted to heavy weapon groups should qualify in heavy weapons as follows:—

Officers and SNCOS	Section Commanders standard in both MMG and 3 inch Mortar.
Corporals	Fire Controllers standard in both weapons.
Marines	Marines standard in both weapons.

Training is similar to that in the infantry except that the jeep and trailer replaces the universal carrier. Carriage by carrier manpack is taught. Amphibious training comprises the landing and haulage of heavy weapons and their ammunition in rock landings and cliff assault.

Assault Engineers

100. Ranks drafted to assault engineer sections are trained in the following:—
(a) Laying and lifting of mines and booby-traps
(b) Simple demolitions
(c) Preparation and destruction of obstacles

(d) Cliff haulage

(e) Preparation of field work

(f) Preparation of forward routes and jeep tracks

(g) Rafting and watermanship for river crossings

(h) Flame warfare

(j) ABC warfare.

(k) Water supply in the field and drainage

(l) Repository (*i.e.,* Derricks, sheerlegs, gins and tackles).

Training is similar to that in the Infantry Battalion Assault Pioneer Platoon, except that cliff haulage and flame warfare duties are added.

Parachutists

101. Sufficient parachute trained ranks should be available within a commando brigade to form one composite troop with a detachment of heavy weapons, signals, and a medical section. Parachutists are normally distributed throughout the commando and must include members of the Headquarters Troop. Parachutists are trained at the Airborne Forces Depot and Parachute Training Squadron, carrying out the basic course and drops as for drafts to airborne troops.

Cliff Leaders

102. Some NCOs and Marines in each fighting troop are trained to climb as leaders (*see* Part III). Cliff leaders should be selected from those for personality and climbing skill. A high proportion of spare leaders should be kept in training in each troop so that the troop is not incapacitated by casualties and so that young climbers are encouraged to develop their skill and leadership. Cliff leaders are trained to climb, as opposed to scaling with an established rope, to use rope projection apparatus and to reconnoitre and prepare scaling routes for assaulting troops. To lead in an assault however, a man requires, as well as climbing ability, the mental capacity for leadership. Stage II training is a potential leaders course and will produce a man who, with additional training and experience in climbing and leadership, is likely to become a cliff leader. This additional training may take place in the unit or on return to Commando School,

but it should be understood that only the exceptional man can become a climbing leader before he has gained some unit experience.

Snipers

103.   Some marines in each fighting troop are trained as snipers. From these men, section and troop snipers and commando sniper sections will be selected for personality and skill. Spare snipers should be kept in training in each troop, so that young shots are encouraged to develop their skill and determination. Snipers are trained at the Small Arms School RM to pass the tests described in Small Arms Training, Vol. I, Pamphlet 23. On completing this course, a man is in effect a potential sniper, whose shooting and fieldcraft will be of considerable value in a fighting troop and who may eventually graduate to a Sniper Section.

Landing Craft Helmsman

104.   Some marines in each fighting troop are trained as landing craft. helmsmen, qualified to take charge of landing craft as helmsmen in sea or river operations. They are trained at the Amphibious School RM and the Commando Training Flotilla in the standard helmsmen course which includes rock landings.

Night and Guerilla Specialists

105.   Marines in each fighting troop are specially trained in observation and movement at night, in unarmed combat, close quarter fighting with sten, pistol and grenade, and patrolling in small numbers. They are trained at the Commando School RM. A fully qualified specialist should reach a minimum of Yellow Belt grading in judo.

Swimmer Canoeists

106.   Sufficient officers, NCOs and marines in each commando are trained swimmer-canoeists to man one special boat section. The equipment for one special boat section is carried in Commando Brigade Stores Park.

Special Courses for Backward Men

107. Under the certain conditions a special Stage II course may be justified for backward men. This course is aimed directly at building character and self-reliance, together with any necessary improvements in physique. It comprises:—

  (a) Progressive athletics to pass standard tests.
  (b) Boxing and/or judo. Physical training, ropework and elementary rock climbing.
  (c) Additional map reading and cross-country work based on two man expeditions and culminating in a one or two weeks supervised expedition in mountain country.

To achieve success the course must be under an instructor with more than average powers of leadership. It would be suitable in war for men returned to training. It is not at present in use and backward men are back squadded in Stage I or earlier training instead.[14]

---

[14] In 2021, recruits who require extra training are back-trooped. Those who are injured are sent to Hunter Company, the rehabilitation department for Commando Training Wing.

CHAPTER 10—TRAINING OF SIGNALLERS, CLERKS, COOKS AND TRADESMEN

108. Signallers, clerks, cooks and tradesmen are, in the Royal Marines, mustered in the technical branch. With the exception of specially enlisted tradesmen, these men undergo normal recruit training, including Stage I Commando Training, before technical training. For service in commandos, it is important that this basic training should be periodically. refreshed so that they are able to march, shoot and generally look after themselves in all situations.

109. The technical training of signallers, clerks, cooks and tradesmen in commandos should be generally similar to that of their equivalents in the infantry (Royal Corps of Signals in the case of the Brigade Signal Section), subject to certain modifications described below.

Signallers

110. The Commando Signaller:—
   (a) May have to work over greater ranges;
   (b) must be prepared to carry all equipment if necessary;
   (c) must have a higher standard of knowledge of maintenance, since the Commando Signallers will be more on their own than their opposite numbers in an Infantry branch;
   (d) must know joint procedure so that he can work to the Navy;
   (e) must have a working knowledge of morse flashing and semaphore so that he can supply the beachmaster's communications (paragraph 199).

111.   The training of a Commando Signaller in Stage II of Commando training should therefore include:—

   (a)   special instruction on aerials and propagation, followed by exercises using small sets to work over long distances;

   (b)   training in the operation of all types of equipment which they may be required. to use;

   (c)   battery charging and maintenance of batteries and battery charging equipment;

   (d)   exercises, to include exercises in the field, maintaining wireless watch in all weather, using battery charging equipment and being compelled to do own replacement of valves, etc.;

   (e)   training in joint procedure, morse flashing and semaphore. Exercises with the Navy if possible, using this procedure;

   (f)   a thorough training in waterproofing, with landing exercises to test this, and exercising operators in maintaining and working sets before, during and after waterproofing, and embarking and disembarking with wireless equipment from various landing craft.

112.   The signaller must be one of the fittest men in the commando. He has one of the heaviest packs to carry and he will be required to maintain communications while the fighting forces are resting. Although the line laying technique is the same as in the ordinary Infantry branch, he must be prepared to carry on his back the telephone and cable required.

Clerks

113.   No special technical knowledge is required beyond the ability to function under difficulties and to fight as a rifleman if required.

Cooks

114.   Cooks, especially cook NCOs, should in addition to their normal training, be taught:—

   (a)   The administration of rations for detached parties.

(b) To be able to cook normal rations using petrol cookers and improvised field kitchens.

(c) Be able to prepare a carcass.

(d) Be encouraged to study problems of living off the country, with particular reference to 'local' food in the area of operations.

Drivers

115. Commando drivers should reach a high standard in cross-country driving, driving in and out of landing craft, concealment of vehicles and map-reading. They should be able to maintain their vehicles when detached and understand the basic principles of waterproofing them.

116. A proportion of drivers should be qualified in landing craft driving so that they may be able, if required, to man landing craft in conjunction with landing craft helmsmen (*see* paragraph 104).

CHAPTER 11—ADVANCED TRAINING

Sub-Unit, Unit and Formation Training

117.   Commando sub-units, units and formations are trained as circumstances permit on similar lines to their infantry equivalents. Particular attention should be paid to the following:—

(a)   **Troop Training**
          Field Firing
          Rock Landings and Cliff Assault
          Patrolling
          Night Work
          Detached troop operations on varying transport scales

(b)   **Commando Training**
          Rapid embarkation and disembarkation
          Commando amphibious assaults on difficult coasts
          Movement in manpack and light scale transport
          Co-operation with carrier borne air forces and naval bombardment
          Control of widely separated troops

(c)   **Brigade Training**
          Collection of intelligence
          Planning and control of amphibious operations
          Planning of movements and embarkation

Specialist Training

118.   Provisions should be made for the continued training of both full-time and alternative specialists. It may be possible to combine this with advanced individual training.

Advanced Individual Training

119. 1st and 2nd Stage Commando Training is lengthy by ordinary service standards but nevertheless only occupies a small part of a man's service life. In that time he can be taught to take his place in a commando and he can be introduced to the mental attitude required of a commando marine. It takes far longer to confirm and fix him in that attitude.

120. When a man joins a commando he is subjected to the routine and to some extent to the drudgery of service life. If nothing in particular is done about it and his training is confined to routine lines, he will soon slip back to the apathetic and unalert attitude all too frequently found in the services. Active service or advanced combined training will keep his enthusiasm and spirit keen, but opportunities for these do not always arise.

121. Periods will therefore occur when special measures will be necessary to keep the commando spirit alive by advanced individual training. Opportunities will vary on different stations, what is possible on one may be out of the question elsewhere. Some suggestions are made below, if they are impracticable on some stations, they will at least be of value in directing attention to the requirement, to meet which imagination and ingenuity must be used.

Advanced Competitive Battle Skills

122. There is always room for improvement in marksmanship, field craft, seamanship, route finding, night work and similar battle skills. The alternative specialists will be of value in working up the remainder in their own specialities, and competitions may be helpful in checking results and increasing interest. *See* also Appendix D—Notes on Hardening and Living Out.

Sport

123. Sports with some service connections such as boxing, wrestling, swimming cross country running and competition shooting are of obvious

value. So also are those which produce self-reliance and initiative such as sailing, cycling, walking and mountaineering.

Mountaineering and Expeditions Generally

124. History shows a strong affinity between mountaineering and irregular warfare. This is partly because mountains are good places for the guerilla; but mountaineers have been successful in the desert and jungle as well as in their chosen hills and have proved that the mental qualities developed by mountaineering are of great worth in warfare elsewhere.

125. Expeditions in mountains or in other desolate country are therefore valuable in fostering the mentality and skills required of commando troops. They may be made in military sub-units or in specially formed groups or teams. The latter are of value in encouraging men to think and fend for themselves rather than to depend sheeplike on officers and NCOs for all forethought and providence.

126. While military exercises in this type of country are valuable, the value of expeditions lies in the fact that men are measuring themselves against natural forces. This value may be lost if there is too much insistence in imposing imaginary battle situations.

127. Cliff leaders may undertake expeditions on rock faces and may initiate others to climbing, but rock climbing is not an essential part of mountain expeditions and a great deal of value can be obtained without difficult, or even without any, rock climbing. Expeditions in mountains under deep snow should only be made under qualified guidance.

128. Failing the availability of mountains, it may be possible to arrange desert or sub-arctic expeditions.

Boating and Seamanship

129. Anything which increases confidence and skill in seamanship is of value. A great deal can be done by pulling and sailing races and day

boating generally. However, more prolonged expeditions under sail or power are naturally of greater value in developing self-reliance. What has been said above about mountain expeditions is also true of sea expeditions.

Attachments to other Arms and Services

130.　Attachments to other arms and services broaden the mind and make for intelligent co-operation. A characteristic of a good commando unit is that all ranks take an intelligent interest in what is going on, therefore attachments should not be limited to officers only.

Initiative Tests

131.　Initiative tests which require lifts to be cadged or affrontery in approaching strangers should be avoided. They tend to encourage the wide boy rather than the good soldier. On the other hand, tests which call for real ingenuity, alertness or observation are of real value.

CHAPTER 12—RESERVE TRAINING

132. Training in the reserve cannot cover adequately everything that is required of a commando marine. The essentials for commando training have been described in previous chapters and comprise basic infantry skill, commando skill, and moral qualities. Basic infantry skill alone could occupy all the time available for reserve training and still be far from complete. Commando skill and moral qualities cannot however be ignored. Not only are they essential to maintain interest and enthusiasm, but unlike much of basic soldiering, they are of slow growth and cannot be covered in an intensive course after mobilisation.

133. In practice, training in moral qualities and in commando skills cannot be separated. For example, cliff climbing helps to instil courage and self-confidence, and cross-country expeditions teach both self-reliance and map-reading. Nor is it advisable to exclude basic soldiering, as men must relate their advanced training to the realities of warfare.

134. For these reasons, reserve training at all stages should comprise:—
   (a) Basic infantry training to the extent necessary to reach limited standards in drill, weapon training and fieldcraft.
   (b) Advanced training in which commando skill and moral qualities are taught together.

135. Drill, weapon training, fieldcraft, elementary tactics on the sand table, and elementary training in commando skill, should as far as possible

be dealt with in evening drills, thus making weekend training available for more advanced commando training. Annual training should be employed on work which cannot be done during the rest of the year, such as amphibious training, field firing, advanced expeditions and certain specialist training. It will however usually be advisable to do a certain amount of basic training at this time to take advantage of the continuity which is not otherwise available.

136.   Reservists should include a normal quota of specialists, but facilities for training reservist specialists vary greatly and considerable reliance must be placed on specialist training which has been done when the reservist was serving with the colours.

137.   For mobilisation, all reservists will be divided into two classes:—
  (a)   Those fit for immediate service in formed units.
  (b)   Those requiring additional training before such service.

138.   The volunteer reserve is composed of men in many different branches of civilian life, who can contribute much of value to the individualist and versatile character of commandos. The remarks in paragraphs 132–134 above are particularly important to these men as they will not join the reserve nor, if they do join it, become enthusiasts if training is limited to elementary soldiering.[15]

139.   Although the volunteer reserve is not primarily a leader training unit, the problem of finding officers and NCOs is a most difficult one in war and men who have undertaken voluntary training in peace are an obvious first source of leader material. Efforts should therefore be made to train as many men as possible for higher rank in war and to record them as suitable for it.

---

[15]   The Royal Marine Reserve was created in 1948 and is the Volunteer Reserve force designed to supply Commando-trained personnel to regular Royal Marines units during times of war or national crisis. In 2021, it comprises 600 reservists operating out of four regional HQs: RMR Bristol, RMR London, RMR Merseyside and RMR Scotland.

Rock landing in a seaway

PART III—THE TECHNIQUE OF DIFFICULT ASSAULT LANDINGS

"The surest way to make a successful landing is to go where you are not expected."

WINSTON CHURCHILL.
Paper written in May 1948.[16]
The Second World War, Volume IV.

CHAPTER 13—GENERAL

140. Commando amphibious operations and the factors to be considered in difficult assault landings have been described in Part I. The technique and training of Commandos in beach assault landings does not differ from that of infantry except for minor adjustments of organisation. Part III below describes in detail the technique and training for difficult. assault landings.

141. Difficult assault landings are those made under conditions not practicable to normal infantry. Difficulties which may have to be overcome either singly or in conjunction are:—

> Rock coastlines
> Sea cliffs
> Mud
> Rough weather or surf
> Long voyages in minor landing craft
> Landings alongside moles or quays

142. Rock coastlines, backed by: cliffs or otherwise, are the most frequent of these. Training for rock landings in rough weather and cliff

---

[16] In fact, this quote originates from a paper Churchill wrote in early May 1943 (not May 1948) while aboard the ocean liner *Queen Mary* en route to the Anglo-American *Trident* conference in Washington D.C. See Winston S. Churchill, *The Second World War, Volume IV: The Hinge of Fate,* (London: Cassell & Co Ltd, 1951), p. 703.

assault is part of the standard training of commandos. As a means of overcoming a common type of obstacle, it opens up long stretches of coast line otherwise closed to assaulting troops. Equally important is the fact that it teaches men to be sure-footed and confident in landing from boats under difficult conditions and in crossing obstacles requiring nerve and physical fitness. Troops thus trained can cope with other obstacles, but special training will be desirable and under conditions in which the safety limit is approached will be necessary *(see* paras. 158 and 184).

143. Landings will usually be made at night to secure surprise and such factors as the state of the tide, the phase of the moon and the weather forecast will play an important part in the timing of an operation. In landing any other than very small forces however, the rate at which men and stores can be landed is an important factor and some compromise on conditions which are ideal for surprise but are too slow may be necessary.

CHAPTER 14—ROCK LANDINGS

Introduction

144. The basic technique of rock landings is that a seaworthy and manoeuvrable boat approaches the rocks on a kedge, until the kedge warp is just holding her off against the engine and the force of the seas breaking on the rocks. Each man in the landing party then jumps from the bow on to the rocks, in rough weather choosing his time as the boat surges. The first man carries the painter and once ashore can to some extent steady the boat with it. Troops re-embark in much the same manner, each man jumping for the boat as it surges towards the rocks. The boat is steadied by the painter held by the last man to re-embark.

Craft

145. The primary characteristics of a craft suitable for use in rock landings are: a length of twenty-five to thirty feet, a long overhanging bow wide enough to provide a good jumping platform, a reliable engine with good astern power and quick reversing arrangements and a good kedge anchor with facilities for handling and snubbing the warp. The length allows the stern to be clear of the normal back surge thus avoiding the danger of being pooped. Longer craft are apt to draw too much water and to be unwieldy.

146. Other minor but important requirements are:—

    (a)   Good observation for the coxswain. Ability to see the kedgeman is a great advantage.

(b) Sufficient space aft for the kedge gear and kedgeman, and a strong stern post.

(c) A re-inforced bow and a water-tight compartment forward.

147. The LCP(L) most nearly approaches these characteristics and can be used safely. for rocky landings in a swell of ten feet. The obsolescent 18 foot dory and the 27 foot raiding craft are suitable for landing in swell up to six feet.

148. Crew duties for rock landing are:—

> Coxswain (LCP(L) only)
> Helmsman
> Bowmen
> Kedgemen
> Drivers (LCP(L) only).

The number of bowmen and kedgemen depends on the size of the craft. Two of each are required for LCP(L), one of each for the 18 foot dory. Bowmen are in excess of the normal crew and are usually found from the assaulting troops and continue ashore with them. The bad visibility from the steering position of the LCP(L) necessitates the NCO i/c (Coxswain) commanding from the deck instead of remaining at the helm.

Coxswain and/or Helmsman

149. The helmsman brings his craft in dead slow at an angle of 90° to the swell. If the craft is not at 90° there is a tendency to broach to, especially in craft with a pointed stern. He gives the kedgeman the signal to drop his kedge far enough out to ensure that the angle of the kedge warp is not too steep when the craft reaches the rocks. On the signal of the bowman, the coxswain orders the kedgeman to snub the kedge warp, making due allowance for the stretch of the rope. While the craft is held close to the rocks for the troops to disembark, the engine must be kept going slow ahead, so that the craft strains against the kedge warp; this keeps the bow in position and reduces the strain on the bowman.

Kedgeman or Kedgemen

150. The kedgeman works on the orders of the coxswain as follows:—
   (a)   To drop the kedge—the kedgeman must ensure that the warp runs out freely so that it lies along the bottom.
   (b)   To test the kedge—when two or three boat lengths from the shore to see that the kedge is holding.
   (c)   To snub the kedge.

On retraction the kedgeman hauls in on the warp and is responsible that it does not become entangled with the propellor or rudder. In smaller craft the kedgeman should haul the craft off by himself, without assistance from the engine, until the kedge is aweigh. In larger craft the engine has to be used to aid the kedgeman in pulling out, but with great discretion to prevent the propellor sucking in the slack of the kedge warp.

Bowman

151.   The bowman is responsible for warning the coxswain of underwater obstacles during the run-in. He also signals to the coxswain when the craft is close enough to the rocks for the troops to land. He then immediately leaps ashore with the painter, and hauls taut until the craft is held in the required position. It is not his job to hold the craft in to the shore—the engine does this. His task is to prevent the bow from swinging away from the landing point. Larger craft need two bowmen; the first one leaps ashore with the painter and the second throws all the remaining coils into the sea to prevent them catching in the feet of the following troops. The bowman is a key man and must be extremely nimble and have a sound knowledge of where to direct the craft during the run-in to the shore. He frequently selects the actual rock on which to land and directs the coxswain accordingly.

152.   In the LCP(L) the troops are sealed inside the craft while at sea. Careful control and organization is necessary for landing so that no time is wasted and the stability and handling of the craft not endangered by the movement of the troops.

153.   The troops jump for the rocks as the craft comes roughly level with it on each upsurge. This is an art which requires much practice

and nerve in a heavy swell. One timid man may delay the landing for many minutes and so jeopardise the craft by holding her too long in a dangerous position. Speed is vitally important; the shorter the time that the craft is held in position, the better.

Re-embarkation

154. Much the same thing applies to re-embarkation; troops should step lightly aboard as the craft comes up on the upward surge. A heavy footed man jumping on the bow on the downward swing might well go right through the deck of an LCP(L). Re-embarkation is generally easier as the troops are jumping on to a known platform, but this also needs agility and confidence.

Choice of Landing Place

155. It is already apparent from the paragraphs above that a clear approach and steep rocks falling into deep water are the ideal. These conditions are in the main more likely to be found at points rather than in bays. Other considerations being equal, the temptation to go for more shelter in a small indentation or bay should be avoided as off-shore rocks, currents and confused seas from the back surge are more probable. Points are frequently more easy to identify at night than bays.

156. Where the landing is to be followed by a cliff assault, the selection of the landing point must be worked out in conjunction with the selection of routes up the cliff. Both of course are subordinate to tactical considerations. It is unwise to choose a landing point more than a few yards from the routes up, since traversing along the rocks with a number of troops at night can be a very slow business.

The Beachmaster—Beach Markings

157. The beachmaster (see para. 199) must attend to each individual craft to direct it to the exact landing place. He should be assisted by a beach party which must signal not only the exact spot, but also give him

a transit for the line of approach to keep clear of underwater obstacles. Normal beach signs should be used, modified if necessary, for ease in handling. Lights should be shone downwards and never towards the coxswain as this blinds him and makes him unable to see when he is approaching a rock. The limits of the landing place must be marked by day or night, since a transit on steep ground has little depth and cannot be followed accurately.

158.   The limiting factors are:—

(a)   **Outlying Rocks.** Outlying rocks are a source of danger at night and can only be avoided by dead slow speed together with the sharp eyes of experienced bowmen and good co-operation between them and the coxswain. It will sometimes be possible for canoeists to mark a clear channel before the operation.

(b)   **Shelving Rocks.** Successful landing depends on a fairly steep-to shore and becomes impracticable on a coastline of gradually shelving reefs. At the other extreme, a vertical cliff running right into the sea without a shelf near the water would also be impracticable.

(c)   **Cross-swell.** A swell running parallel to the coast makes landing difficult but it is usually possible to choose a landing place to avoid it.

(d)   **Weather.** It is difficult to judge accurately the limits of practicable weather. At a suitable landing place with good boats and well trained men, landing and re-embarkation can be done in a swell up to 10 feet.

Intelligence

159.   The chief requirement is for air photographs to be taken at low tide and of a scale of 1 : 10,000 or larger. If possible photographs at several stages of tide and with a swell running should be used. Rough weather photographs are valuable for revealing under water obstacles. Large scale charts are another important requirement.

160. Reconnaissance by canoe is possible in a swell up to five feet. If by this means the approach and actual landing points can be marked, any risk of failure is greatly reduced.

Special Precautions

161. Among other precautions the following should be noted:—
- (a) **Holding Ground.** If the kedge does not hold, the boat becomes unmanageable as soon as she enters broken water. Kedges should be chosen to suit the bottom expected. In mixed rock and sand a Danforth anchor is probably the best type at present.
- (b) **Length of Kedge Warp.** The depth of water close to landing places must be calculated and kedge warps must be long enough to work in this depth, making due allowance for swell and under estimation.
- (c) **Spare Kedges.** If craft are required to come in a second time to withdraw troops spare kedges should be available.
- (d) **Spare Craft.** In a raid spare craft should be available to take the place of any becoming unserviceable.

Training

162. A high standard of training is required from boat crews and assaulting troops. In the later stages they must train together. Mistakes with serious consequences are far more commonly made by crews, and their thorough training and briefing is vital.

Numbers 1 and 2 climbers

CHAPTER 15—CLIFF ASSAULT

163. For purposes of assault, cliffs are divided into:—

(a) Cliffs which active and well trained troops can scramble up without complicated aids.

(b) Cliffs on which assaulting troops require further assistance:—

    (i) Those which can be climbed by climbers who establish ropes for the main assault.

    (ii) Those which can only be climbed by using projected ropes or scaling ladders.

(c) Cliffs impracticable to troops.

Darkness and height add considerably to the difficulty of a climb and many men feel the need for a rope at 50 to 100 feet on a slope which would not trouble them lower down. Furthermore a margin of error must be allowed for cliffs which cannot be tested by actual climbing in advance. Subject to this, unnecessary complications should be avoided.[17]

Scramble Assaults

164. Most cliffs are either sloped well back from the vertical or present a broken face through and up which routes can be found. The possibility that such easy faces and gullies will be wired, mined or watched, must be considered. Subject to detours ordered to avoid particular dangers, troops can use the easiest routes up on a pre-determined frontage, provided

---

[17] Prior to the D-Day landings in June 1944, several Royal Marine Commando units were trained in cliff assault techniques at the Commando Snow and Mountain Warfare Training Centre (CSMWTC) based in St Ives, Cornwall. Post-war, these skill-sets and professional knowledge were perpetuated by the Commando Cliff Assault Centre (CCAC), and later by the Cliff Assault Wing (CAW).

no bunching or congestion occurs. Under these conditions, control is maintained by sub-section commanders or troop subalterns, choosing their route in accordance with previous orders and leading their men up.

165.   Men must be fit and sure-footed in order to move fast in daylight or silently at night on steep ground. They should wear lightly nailed boots (see Appendix G). Leaders may find it convenient to fix short lengths of rope, or even at night to lay a continuous rope or tape as a guide, but on most of the route men will be unaided and will follow closely behind their leader and not wait for him to complete the climb before following him up the cliffs.

166.   A short section of steep unbroken cliff is sometimes found at the top or bottom of a long scramble. This may be overcome:—
    (a)   By cliff leaders preparing ropes as for a steep cliff assault on the bad sections only.
    (b)   By providing throwing grapnels or 2 inch mortar grapnels with leading troops.

167.   Trained cliff leaders (see para. 169) with equipment, should if possible be available in reserve at troop headquarters in order to assist:—
    (a)   If the cliff turns out more difficult than forecast.
    (b)   If assaulting sections are forced to take more difficult routes to avoid fire, mines or wire.

Scaling Assaults

168.   On cliffs which are too steep for scrambling, aids must first be established by selected men before the main assaulting force can scale. There are four ways of doing so:—
    (a)   **Climbing Leaders**—if possible one pair per section climbing the cliff and establishing ropes.
    (b)   **Projection**—rockets or mortars are used to shoot grapnels up the cliff carrying ropes or ladders.
    (c)   **Scaling Ladders**
    (d)   **Parachutists or Agents**

Climbing Leaders

169. Cliff leaders are trained in rock climbing and in finding and preparing routes for the main assault. They work in pairs, Number 1 leading the climb, Number 2 assisting him and bringing up a second rope. The leaders secure their ropes to grip-fasts at the cliff top, see that they are run over the best available route for scaling, and defend the cliff head until the main body arrives. Climbing leaders carry a throwing grapnel for short overhangs, which sometimes occur at the cliff top.

170. The advantages and disadvantages of climbing leaders are:—
    (a)   They are silent.
    (b)   They do not require heavy complicated gear.
    (c)   On steep unbroken cliffs it is difficult to tell without trying whether a climb will go, therefore a large margin of safety must be allowed on operations in which climbs have been selected from air photographs, etc., and only climbs which have promise of being not more than "Difficult" can be undertaken unless the party is prepared to cancel the operation and turn back.
    (d)   They can operate on quarter or brighter moonlight or in complete darkness by the use of lamps attached to the climber's head. These are not easily detected.

Projection

171. The methods at present available for projection are:—
    (a)   **2 inch Mortar Grapnel.** A grapnel bomb with a $1\frac{1}{2}$ inch rope, for cliffs up to 90 feet, fired from a standard 2 inch Mortar.
    (b)   **3 inch Mortar Grapnel.** A grapnel bomb with $1\frac{1}{2}$ inch rope, for cliffs up to 150 feet, fired from a standard 3 inch Mortar.
    (c)   **6 Pdr Schermuly Rocket.** Carrying a $1\frac{1}{2}$ inch rope, for cliffs up to 150 feet, fired from an expendable discharger.

(d) **Mk IV 2 inch Rocket.** Carrying a rope ladder for over-hanging cliffs up to 130 feet, fired from a special stand.

172.   The advantages and disadvantages of projection methods are:—

(a)   Cliffs impossible to climb can be scaled, provided they offer sufficient footholds for the legs to give some assistance to the arms pulling on the rope. Short overhangs can be scaled by rope ladders, but this is very slow.

(b)   Ropes are established quickly. The 2 inch Mortar and 6 Pdr Schermuly rocket can be fired from any landing craft before the troops land and scaling can then start immediately the leading troops have landed and tested the ropes. The 3 inch Mortar can be fired from the LCA.

(c)   They are noisy. Rockets are more likely to be detected than mortars, the noise and the flash of the mortars being instantaneous and made at sea level where they are reflected seaward by the cliffs.

(d)   They require reasonably accurate aiming and are one or two shot weapons. Some margin of safety may be given by firing a salvo and by having a high proportion of ropes and grapnels in reserve.

(e)   Sufficient light is required to aim by. If the cliffs are silhouetted and navigation is accurate, bright starlight would be adequate.

Scaling Ladders

173.   Low vertical or overhung cliffs up to about 20 feet can be scaled by light hand carried ladders, preferably of aluminium or alloy. The method is silent and quick but the height limitation is very severe. The possibility of using ladders for short unclimbable pitches in an otherwise easy climb should not be overlooked.

174.   A power-driven Merryweather fire ladder has been fixed on a DUKW and can be used to scale cliffs up to 80 feet in height. The method is dependent on DUKWs or similar amphibians being carried

3-in. mortar with grapnel bomb loaded showing bridle attachments. Spare bomb leaning on rope box

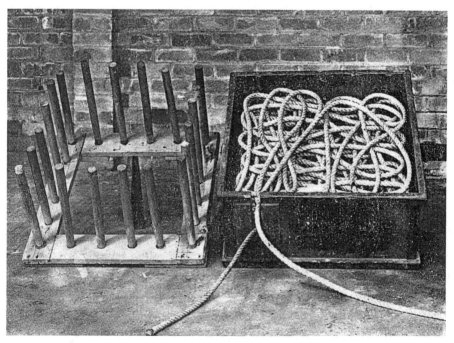

Rope box and pin case

to the scene of the assault and on the presence of a beach up to the foot of the cliff. The DUKW carrying the ladder is rather top heavy and not as seaworthy as a normally loaded DUKW.

Parachutists or Agents

175.   It may be possible to arrange for previously dropped parachutists or agents, introduced by whatever means are available, to prepare the way. The great disadvantage of their use is the possibility of early discovery and loss of surprise. Helicopters might possibly be used with advantages and disadvantages similar to parachutists.

Tactical Organisation of a Cliff Assault

176.   It will be apparent that the initial phases of a cliff assault may comprise:—

(a)   Initial reconnaissance by canoe parties, marking landing places and finding routes.

(b)   Establishment of routes by climbing, projection, or ladders, by advanced parties who thereafter hold the cliff head until the main body arrives.

(c)   Scaling by the main body of assault troops.

(d)   Further organisation of routes for the follow up by reserves and the establishment of haulage for heavy weapons and administration. (*See* Chapter 17).

All these phases will not necessarily occur in every assault, indeed a simple plan is most important. For example, in a scramble assault, (*b*) and (*c*) are combined in one phase.

177.   The organisation of waves for landing will depend on circumstances, but for cliffs more than about 50 feet, it will save congestion at a very vulnerable time if the advance parties (*see* para. 176 (*b*)) are landed ahead of the main body of assaulting troops. The latter can either be called in or come in on a time programme. At night the landing of the advance party may be undetected and there may therefore be a considerable

amount of time available for establishing routes. In daylight however a great deal will depend on speed and the advance parties will be required to have the routes ready in the minimum time possible.

178. It may be desirable to provide some fire support with the advanced parties to prevent interference with their climb by chance patrols and to help them hold the cliff head. The scaling of high cliffs against organised enemy fire is not practicable.

Withdrawal

179. Established routes can be used for withdrawal or new routes made. Roping down by mountaineering methods allows rapid descent of cliffs if troops are thoroughly practiced in it. Withdrawal routes should be organised for speed on similar lines to those described in paragraph 183 below:

Selection of Routes of Ascent

180. The selection of a suitable landing place must of necessity take precedence in the choice of routes up the cliff. Unless there is an easy beach a coastal traverse over rocks at night from the landing point to the climbs should be avoided. It is usually better to compromise and accept a worse cliff with a good landing place.

181. In the selection of the routes of ascent themselves the following should be considered:—

(a) Rapid build-up is important.

(b) It may be necessary in the interest of silence and thus of surprise for the advance parties to avoid the gulleys, where loose stones congregate and which are obvious routes, and to take harder climbs. Once the cliff top is secured, faster routes can be prepared.

(c) Where there is a choice of routes or where there is doubt whether a route is practicable, the cliff leaders who are to find the way should be consulted in the planning stage.

(d) Cover from fire at the bottom and on the cliff, also of a suitable defensive position at the top.

(e) As in crossing any obstacle a cliff assault should be made on as wide a front as possible and as many routes as possible brought into use.

182. The speed of ascent will vary greatly with the height, slope and texture of the obstacle. Thus it is only possible to give a rough rule of thumb. It should not take a man roping up in the assault longer than 5 minutes per 100 feet. Under favourable conditions 3 minutes for 100 feet can be achieved at night.

183. Leaders establishing assault routes by whatever means should not content themselves with the chance fall of their rope but should plan and lay out routes, as far as they can in the time available, to make them straightforward and fast for the main body. Factors to be considered are:—

(a) **Steepness and Overhangs.** Troops with their battle equipment cannot rope up more than a few feet of overhang or about 100 feet of really steep cliff. They can do much greater heights if there are intervening easy pitches. Difficult roping-up pitches can often be turned by a well-planned route.

(b) **Number of Ropes.** When roping up very steep slopes only one man may be on the rope at a time. On sloping cliffs however two or three may be on the same rope. Generally the more ropes the faster the force will get up. Additional ropes can be provided:—

(i) In parallel—*i.e.*, more routes.

(ii) In series—*i.e.*, two or more successive ropes each separately secured on one route so that a second man can start on rope one when the first reaches rope two.

Method (ii) is important on long climbs which are too steep to permit more than one man on a rope, and should be considered for climbs over about 80 feet.

(c) **Easy Pitches.** On a long climb there may be easy pitches on which roping will be unnecessary. Taping will probably be necessary to lead troops from the top of one rope to the bottom of the next; or a hand rope fixed at both ends laid, by which troops can steady themselves but which they need not wait for the man ahead to clear before starting.

(d) **Size of Rope.** A 1 1 inch rope is normally used for roping up and down. On very high steep cliffs, or where troops are not trained, a 2 or 24 inch rope may be used with advantage for roping up only. These ropes are too thick to permit rapid roping down. As weight is an important factor and there is not very great strain on the rope, the use of coir rope is worth consideration.

(e) **Assistance.** If there is a bad overhang or other awkward place a lightly equipped man should stand by to assist heavily loaded or less skilled men on it. The No. 2 leader is available for this work.

The factors should be considered at the detailed planning stage and leaders briefed in their work.

Limit Conditions

184. Factors which in conjunction may make a cliff impracticable to assault are:—

(a) **Height.** The limits of projection and scaling are definite, but there is no limit to the height that can be climbed provided the cliff is climbable. The limits of roping-up are also indefinite, subject to the factors described in paragraph 183 above.

(b) **Steepness.** Climbing and roping-up is impracticable near or beyond the vertical.

(c) **Type of Rock.** Steep rocks can be climbed if they are sound and have holds which may be small but must be there. Loose rock or earth can be climbed if it is not too steep, and can be roped-up provided it is set back from the vertical.

(d) **Time.** On practicable but high cliffs or for operations requiring more than one commando troop, time may be a limiting factor.

As a rough rule therefore, steep cliffs of loose rock or very smooth hard rocks are impracticable beyond the maximum height for projection; steep cliffs which are sound enough to climb are practicable within the limit of roping-up less steep cliffs, even if unsound, are practicable up to any height.

Training

185.   A standardised procedure which may be useful in general training is given at Appendix E, but it must be clearly understood that it should never form the basis of operational planning. Each operation must be judged on its own merits and a procedure worked out and rehearsed for the particular problems presented.

186.   A commando troop, including its cliff leaders, can be refreshed in cliff assault training and brought up to operational standards in three weeks or at a bare minimum in a fortnight.

CHAPTER 16—MISCELLANEOUS DIFFICULTIES

Beach Landings in Rough Weather and Surf

187. Landings in ocean surf may be made in LCP(L) or amphibians, the latter being essential when there is an outlying reef on which landing craft ground. Special training is required.

188. Apart from such extreme conditions, surf caused by rough weather and swell may occur on any coastline. The length of the landing craft plays an important part in fixing limiting conditions, but troops and crews should be trained to use their craft to the best advantage.

189. For crews, this amounts to keeping control of the boat in broken water, preventing her from broaching to, and getting her off using a kedge if necessary.

190. Troops require practice to make them, with their equipment and weapons, handy in the boat, confident and quick in jumping out when she grounds, and able to steady her and shove her off when necessary. Re-embarkation is more difficult than landing, as the boat is increasing in draught and will stick unless kept well out. Consequently troops will have to wade out, steady the boat, and help each other up her side. There is nothing complicated in all this, but practice, good leadership and teamwork between troops and crews are required to do it well.

191. For landing small parties in rough weather, special light pulling boats have been used. They have however many obvious disadvantages. If used, everyone in the boat must be specially trained to pull an oar in

surf, the boat being carried up the beach and remaining ashore until re-embarkation.

Mud

192. Soft mud may be negotiated by troops wearing pattens or using special sleds. It has not at present been possible to produce standard specifications or training methods.

Long Voyages in Minor Landing Craft

193. The danger of radar detection or of mines described in Part I, or other reasons, may make it necessary for the lowering position to be a considerable distance from the coast. A 20 mile run-in is not improbable. In a 12 knot LCP(L) on a direct course this would take 1 hour 40 minutes with considerable addition for forming up and other manoeuvres. The main difficulties which must be considered in planning are likely to be seasickness and exposure to cold and wet. The counter-measures are fairly obvious; practice, seasick pills, adequate protection and clothing and avoidance of overcrowding by reducing numbers per boat.

Improvised Landing Craft

194. Small parties of troops may have to use improvised landing craft, but the time honoured method of pulling boats should be avoided if there is any possibility of opposition from the beaches. On most beaches small power boats running directly ashore would be far preferable. Troops who are good seamen as well as good soldiers will be a help in this type of work.

Landings alongside Moles or Quays

195. Landings alongside moles or quays set a special problem which must be studied on the merits of each case. The two. vital factors are likely to be:—

(a) The possibility of getting and keeping the ship or landing craft close alongside.

(b) The relative heights of deck and quayside or mole.

Miscalculations in either of these factors will lead almost certainly to disaster.

196. There will usually be both a horizontal and vertical gap between deck and quayside and the difficulty will probably be aggravated by movement of the ship and possibly by barbed wire or other obstacles. Ramps, scaling ladders or other adaptations of cliff assault methods and wall scaling will be necessary to overcome this difficulty. Whatever means are used, it will be extremely important to keep the troops lightly equipped and to have them shod in footwear which will help them to be sure-footed. To send men to fight under these conditions weighted down with equipment is inexcusable. The question of footwear (*see* Appendix G) is more difficult and must be given close attention.

197. A detailed historical account of planning this type of operation may be found in "The Raid on Zeebrugge" by Captain A. F. B. Carpenter, V.C., R.N.[18]

---

[18] The Zeebrugge raid on 23 April 1918 (St George's Day) involved storming parties drawn from the 4th Battalion, The Royal Marines. Embarked on the old Cruiser HMS *Vindictive*, as well as aboard two converted ferries, HMSs *Daffodil* and *Iris*, the Marines' job was to storm the Belgian port's mole and neutralise German coastal gun positions placed upon it. This was in direct support of the Royal Navy who attempted to close the entrance to the harbour (an Imperial German Navy U-Boat facility) by means of block ships. Despite incurring heavy casualties and failing to seal-off the port entrance, the raiders delivered a great morale boost to the British nation and enhanced the reputation of the Royal Navy and Royal Marines at a critical juncture in World War I.

CHAPTER 17—FOLLOW-UP AND ADMINISTRATION

Landing Place Organisation and Control

198. The landing of the assault wave by the methods so far described will be under normal tactical control. This may be all that is required for small operations of short duration, but in larger or more prolonged operations, the assaulting troops will be followed by reserves, heavy weapons, ammunition and stores. It will then be necessary:—

(a) To decide which landing place or places should, in view of physical difficulties and enemy opposition, be used for the follow-up troops.

(b) To utilise all available resources in making such places practicable for heavy weapons and stores.

(c) To establish control over landing craft, troops and stores to be landed and to put through the landing programme against the inevitable difficulties.

In the case of cliff assault, the landing and route up the cliff must be considered together.

199. Under conditions of difficult landings, it will be necessary to establish unified control of the landing places by an officer who combines the duties of Beachmaster. and Military Landing Officer, and who can appreciate and deal with in combination seaward and shoreward problems. He will require communications, landing craft control personnel, shore control personnel and assault engineers.

Methods of Landing Stores

200.   Methods of handling heavy weapons and stores which should be considered are:—

(a)   **Manpack**

3-inch Mortars and MMG, their ammunition and that for troop weapons, explosives and other stores can be broken down into man packs and carried ashore by men landing by methods similar to those employed by the assaulting troops. Heavy weapons groups will usually carry their own weapons ashore, and demolition parties the stores they require. Ammunition for heavy weapons and additional demolition stores may be carried by reserve troops. Assistance in landing and in cliff scaling may be required for heavily loaded men, the roller method, *see* Appendix I, may be useful for the latter. If further ammunition or stores are required, it will probably be best to establish special landing and porter parties between landing place and forward dumps.

(b)   **Ropeway**

If there is a cliff or high ground near the coast, it may be possible to erect a ropeway. In a good holding ground, the seaward end of the ropeway may run to an anchor. The load is then lifted direct from the landing craft. A power-worked ropeway can be rigged in about an hour and maintain a lift of 6 tons an hour with a maximum single lift of about 4 cwt. (*see* Appendix I). It is much preferable to one worked by man power which requires a considerable working party.

(c)   **Seizure of Minor Beach or Landing Place**

On difficult coasts there are often gaps in the cliffs, rocks or other obstacles. Such gaps are likely to be watched or guarded and are usually unsuitable for direct assault. A flank or rear assault by light troops landed to a flank may have much better chances of success and be able to open the way for stores and even vehicles to be landed. If vehicles are landed they are likely to be very few and firm planning and control will be necessary.

(d) **Airdrop**

It may be possible to drop stores or even vehicles by air, although conditions which permit any considerable airdrop will often indicate that the whole operation should be done by air. However, this will not always be true as the requirements for dropping assaulting forces are considerably more demanding than those for dropping essential stores. Airdropping may therefore be a very great help to a commando force landing on a difficult coast, but it would be unrealistic to suppose that large airdrops will always be available under conditions which rule out airborne assault.

Casualty Evacuation

201.   It is possible to evacuate small numbers of casualties down a cliff by roller assistance or from cliff to sea by aerial ropeway. For any considerable evacuation scheme some form of beach or artificial landing place will be required. An aid post capable of holding wounded and giving them immediate treatment, while awaiting the establishment of an evacuation route, will be necessary.

Administration in General

202.   In view of the difficulties of landing loads, administrative support will have to be confined to essentials; very possibly to the supply of ammunition and explosive stores and the collection of wounded, pending the opening of an evacuation route. Troops may have to depend on their own resources for food, water and warmth; and this with only very light loads to be carried in the assault. Commando troops should therefore be trained to fend for themselves for limited periods. (*See* Appendix D). If it is intended to live off the country for longer periods, proper planning, control and organisation of requisitioning will be important not only to maintain discipline, but to conserve resources. The problem should be the subject of an administrative appreciation during the planning stages and dealt with realistically, not left to chance. The impressment of vehicles may form part of the administrative plan.

APPENDIX A

SOME CHARACTERISTICS OF SHIPPING SUITABLE FOR RAIDING OPERATIONS

SHIPS

1.   **LSI (M).** Light fast passenger steamers converted for use in assault landings by fitting troop decks and strengthened davits.

      Typical characteristics are:—

Tonnage	4000–6000 gross
Speed	20–22 knots
Endurance	Varies very greatly
Troop Capacity	200–400
Hoisting Capacity	6–8 LCP(L) or LCA

2.   **Destroyers.** The following outline characteristics of the Battle Class are cited as an example:—

Tonnage	2,400
Troop Capacity	60–80 for short voyages
Speed	35 knots
Hoisting Capacity	3 27ft. raiding craft (SN 8) or similar boats. Could be increased to 4 by fitting an additional pair of davits. Up to 4 20ft. raiding craft (SN 6) or 18ft. dories can be carried on the upper deck and hoisted out on torpedo davits.

3.   **Fast Patrol Boats.** (Formerly MTB and MGB). FPBs, of which there are two types, the Long and the Short, are very effective for making raids in the dark hours, especially if radio counter measures are used, owing

to their high speed and small silhouette. They can make a reasonably silent approach and their small draft enables them to cross-minefields and to reach positions close inshore where other types of surface craft may be unable to go. They are restricted by bad weather as regards the state of sea but can be safely operated in low visibility. In daylight hours they are vulnerable to attack by fighters unless provided with adequate air cover. Cooking and accommodation facilities are poor and troops must be prepared to rough it and prepare their own food. FPBs are not themselves suitable for beaching, and disembarkation must be by dory or canoe.

Typical characteristics:—

Long FPB

Length	About 115 feet
Speed maximum cont.	24¼ knots
,, cruising	22 knots
Endurance	400–600 miles at cruising speed
Troop Capacity	20
Hoisting Capacity	One 20 foot raiding craft or 18 foot dory

Short FPB

Length	About 73 feet
Speed maximum cont.	31 knots
,, cruising	25 knots
Endurance	400 miles at 25 knots
Troop Capacity	10
Hoisting Capacity	As for Longs

4. **Submarines.** The following outline characteristics of the A and S Classes are cited as an example:—

Tonnage	700/1620 tons
Maximum speed	14–18 knots
Troop capacity	12
Hoisting Capacity	Mk lx canoes or inflatables up to full troop capacity.

APPENDIX B

SOME CHARACTERISTICS OF LANDING CRAFT SUITABLE FOR RAIDING OPERATIONS

1.　**LCP(L).** Unarmoured, but faster and more seaworthy than the LCA. They are suitable for rock and rough weather landings. The present design is obsolescent.

Weight	Approximately 8 tons
Length	41 feet 4½ inches
Speed (maximum)	10–12 knots
Endurance	170 miles
Capacity	20–25 in addition to crew.

2.　**27 foot Raiding Craft.** Under construction on the basis of the SN 8 fitted with an engine and buoyancy gear. The following figures are estimates only:—

Weight	Approximately 2 tons
Speed	6 knots
Capacity	10 in addition to crew.

3.　**20 foot Raiding Craft.** Under construction on the basis of an engined SN 6.

Weight	7 cwt.
Speed	3½ knots
Capacity	8

4.　**18 foot Dory**

Speed	6 knots
Capacity	5 fully equipped men in addition to crew.

5.   **Canoes**

    Mk lxx   2 man general purpose
                                     collapsible canoe
    Mk IIxx   3 man reconnaissance canoe
    Mk IX   2 man powered canoe

6.   **Inflatables**

At present there are three types of inflatables:—

    Y Type   2 man
    RAF Type D   5 man
    RAF Type Q   7 man

These may eventually be placed by two designs, one small and one large.

APPENDIX C
NOTES ON MAN LOADS

General Principles

1.   The optimum marching load for the average man is not more than one third of his body weight, although with training and the right equipment heavier loads can be carried. This load however is for *marching* not for fighting, and it should be appreciated that:—

    (a)   Mobile, active, aggressive fighting on foot is not physically possible to heavily loaded men.

    (b)   Apart from the physical factor, fear and fatigue are the same in their moral effect on an advance. When a man is tossed into combat carrying such weight that his shoulders and his knees shake, he has lost his main chance to conquer quickly his early fear, usually his worst.

    It is therefore important not to confuse loads which can satisfactorily be carried on the march with loads which can be taken into battle.

2.   The solution for normal infantry is straight forward to the extent that vehicles can be used to reduce the weight on the man. In commando operations there may be no vehicles at all and they are always likely to be scarce.

3.   It will therefore be necessary to have two, or perhaps three scales:—

    (a)   The fighting scale.

    (b)   The marching scale.

    (c)   Possibly the porterage scale.

    Tactical planning must ensure that men are not caught up in a battle until their marching scale has been dumped.

4.   In an assault landing, fighting is likely from the moment the first waves land. It will therefore be necessary to have these waves at fighting scales and the probability that men will get wet on difficult assaults and thus increase their loads must also be considered. In an advance, the advance guard should be on fighting scales, so that it can go instantly into action. There will be a natural reluctance to have two different scales of loading within a force. The administrative staff will look with envy on the fighters, as potential load carriers; the tactician at the load carriers or porters as more potential bayonets. In battle, one aggressive active man is however worth many exhausted or immobile men. More than lip service must be paid to this fact and the distinction between load carriers and fighters kept clear. This is not of course to say that load carriers cannot dump their loads to fight, or that the same set of men remain lightly loaded fighters throughout an operation. Porters may be found from a reserve unit, and a commander may have to accept this temporary loss of fighting power.

5.   Bayonet strength should be kept up by keeping total loads down. The question of what is essential must be tackled afresh in each new operation, and nothing must be included in a load because it is customary or might possibly be useful. Operations without transport are likely to be of limited duration and every item taken must be tested by the question "It is worth risking lives to carry?" The contents of the small pack and even some reserve ammunition are likely to be discarded under this test.

6.   When scales have been made out, it must be a matter of discipline and training that no more load is carried. Men are inclined to add to their loads because they do not understand the reason for keeping loads down.

7.   The change from marching scale to fighting scale should be organised and practiced so that men can come into action quickly. Clear orders should be given as to who is to order dumping, provision being

made for casualties. Dumping will be unnecessary for defensive action or when passing through sporadic fire, but to expect aggressive action without it is to court failure.

8.   The following scales are given as factual examples and are based on a temperate climate. In hot climates they will require reducing but to some extent this will be covered by reductions in clothing and bedding. In cold climates heavier margins must be allowed for clothing, bedding rations and shelter, and the mobility of the force will consequently be reduced.

Fighting Scale

9.   (a)   **Rifle Group**

	lbs.	ozs
Basic clothing	11	5
Waterbottle full	3	13
First field dressing		3
Webbing equipment (less small pack)	1	8
Clasp knife and lanyard		6
WS Tablets		4
TOTAL	17	7

Arms and Ammunition	lbs.	ozs.
Rifle and bayonet and 10 rounds	11	4
50 rounds .303 bandolier	3	5
2 LMG magazines or 2 inch Mortar bombs	5	6
2 grenades	3	0
TOTAL LOAD	40	6

NOTE: A further saving of 9lbs. 8 ozs. may be made by omitting webbing equipment and water bottle. One magazine and one grenade would then be carried in battle dress pockets.

(b) **LMG Group or Mortar Group**	*lbs.*	*Ozs.*
Clothing and equipment as above	17	7
Arms and Ammunition		
LMG or 2 inch Mortar	23	8
5 magazines (1 on gun) or		
5 2 inch Mortar bombs	13	7
	54	6

NOTE: Nos. 2 and 3 of Bren and Mortar groups each carry a rifle and 50 rounds bandolier, spare parts wallet and 4 Bren magazines or 4 2-inch Mortar bombs. The total weight is approximately 54lbs. for each man.[19]

(c) **Ammunition**

(i) Sub-section basis	*Grenades*	*.303 amm.*	*LMG Mags.*	*2 inch Motar Bombs*
Rifle Group (8 men)	16	400	8	8
Bren Group (3 men)	–	100	13	–
TOTAL	16	500	21	8

---

[19] In 1951, the standard issue weapons available to the Royal Marines Commandos were the No.4 .303 Lee Enfield Rifle, the .303 BREN Light Machine Gun, the 9mm STEN sub-machine gun, the .303 Vickers Medium Machine Gun, the 3inch mortar and the 83mm PIAT. In addition, 41 (Independent) Commando RM were issued with the American M1 .30 calibre Garand semi-automatic rifle for service in Korea. In 2021, the Royal Marines are armed primarily with the 5.56mm SA80 rifle, the 5.56mm Colt C8 rifle, the 7.62mm General Purpose Machine Gun, the .50 calibre Browning Machine Gun, the 81mm mortar, the 127mm Javelin anti-tank missile system, the L115A3 snipers rifle and the L129A1 7.62mm Sharpshooter rifle.

(ii) **2 inch Mortar**	Grenades	.303 amm.	2 inch Motar Bombs
Group			
4 sub-sections (provide)	–	–	32
Mortar Group (3 men)	–	100	13
TOTAL	NIL	100	45

NOTE: The above loads do not include a respirator, steel helmet, emergency ration or digging tool.

Marching Scales

10. **Light Scale.** Small pack and 24 hours rations.
Heavy scale. Bergen rucksack and 48 hours rations.

Porterage

11. Porters carry a minimum personal and fighting load with man load using carrier manpack, according to weight (*see* para. 13).

Dress and Equipment	lbs.	ozs.
Battledress	5	6
Shirt, Vest and Pants	2	0
Socks		4
Boots	4	8
Anklets		8
Beret		4
Field Dressing		2
Waterbottle filled	3	13
Pistol and 12 rounds	2	3
TOTAL	19	0

12.   For example of loads capable of being carried by porterage *see* Table A.

Man Pack Equipment

13.   *(a)*   **Small Pack.** Satisfactory for light loads but becomes uncomfortable with over 15–20lbs, on account of the tension of the shoulder straps. Weight 1lb. 8ozs.

    (b)   **Bergen Rucksack.** Its frame and capacious bag is well adapted to carrying a number of separate articles of medium weight. Suitable for loads up to 40–50lbs. Weight 6lbs.

    (c)   **Carrier Manpack.** Metal frame with straps. This is an excellent general purpose carrier, for loads up to and exceeding 50lbs. Weight 4½lbs. Loads should be waterproof as they are not protected from rain and spray.

The Principles of Packing a Load on a Carrier

14.   The centre of gravity of the load should lie between the shoulder blades and close to the back of the frame. The object is achieved by the following methods:—

    (a)   The heavy objects are placed close to the back of the frame.

    (b)   Heavy objects are placed high up.

    (c)   Long objects are carried vertically, not horizontally. The width of the load should

    (d)   not exceed 24 inches.

    (e)   The shape of the load is kept flat as possible.

    (f)   Bulky loads should not be as heavy as compact ones.

The Technique of Carrying Loads

15.   *(a)*   **Adjustment of the shoulder straps.** Shoulder straps should be adjusted so that the pressure of the waist band is not taken in the small of the back, but on the sacrum and pelvis.

    (b)   **Rests.** For loads up to 55 lbs, 10 minutes rest in the hour is recommended and for loads over 60 lbs, 5 minutes every

half hour. During short rests it is wise not to remove a heavy load from the back, but to support it on a bank or rock.

(c) **Pads.** Carriage of the large and small packs imposes a severe strain on the shoulder muscles. This can be alleviated to some degree by the use of felt or rubber shoulder pads. The felt packing from explosive and mortar containers is quite satisfactory for this purpose.

(d) **Speed and rhythm.** Speed should be adjusted to the gradient so as to avoid laboured breathing. Otherwise the pace should be regular and rhythmical.

(e) **Selection of route.** A longer route with an even surface is to be preferred to a short one leading over broken or excessively steep ground.

(f) **Training loads.** During porterage training, loads should be heavier than the normal operational loads.

TABLE A to APPENDIX C

(1) Small Arms Ammunition			(2) Rations			(3) Bedding			(4) 3-inch Mortar and Ammunition		
.303 Bdr 1000 rds	75lb	0oz	14 Man compopacks	62lb	8oz	12 Blankets	50lb	2oz	Tripod	45lb	0oz
or			or			or			or		
3 Boxes of 12 36 grenades	75	0	12 Man compopacks	53	0	24 Lightweight Blankets	58	0	Barrel	44	8
or			or			or			or		
9mm 2000 rds	78	0	7 Gallons water	64	0	24 Gas capes	66	0	Base Plate	37	0
or									or		
24 2-inch Mortar bombs in carriers	60	0							5 3-inch Mortar bombs	50	0

APPENDIX D

NOTES ON HARDENING; LIVING OUT; AND LIVING IN THE FIELD

General

Normal civilised conditions and living indoors softens a man's condition until he can not resist either exposure to cold, or unaccustomed exposure to heat. A man whose body is hardened is more able to resist fatigue and extremes of temperature, and suffers less hardship when the scale of rations is reduced to a minimum.[20]

2.   In order to train men to a hard condition therefore, the two principal factors are:—

(a)   Resistance to exposure.

(b)   Resistance to fatigue.

---

[20]   Appendix D draws heavily upon Combined Operations pamphlet No. 27, *Hardening of Commando Troops for Warfare*, first produced in 1944. The author of this piece of doctrine was retired Royal Naval Medical officer, Surgeon Commander George Murray Levick RN, who had accompanied Captain Robert Falcon Scott on his 1912 Antarctic expedition. Levick was a leading member of staff on the fieldcraft wing of the Special Training Centre at Lochailort, precursor of the Commando Basic Training Centre at Achnacarry. It was at Lochailort that Levick "applied medical and scientific principle to the challenges of fitness, diet and survival for special service troops", expertise he distilled into *Hardening of Commando Troops for Warfare*. Among other things, Levick's handbook addressed "the hardening of the body" against "exposure and fatigue", as well as the "'science of rationing', 'pack marching', 'seasickness and immersion in water' and 'the bivouac".

Resistance to Exposure

3. The problem is to conserve the heat that is produced in the body primarily by the action of the muscles in their combustion of fuel food during activity, and secondly by the organs of the body during the digestion of meals. A knowledge of this fact reveals why men feel chilly in the early hours of the morning when sleeping in the open; the digestion of the evening meal has ceased and very little heat is being produced by the action of the muscles. Nature's solution is to produce the condition of shivering which brings muscles into play and thus produces heat.

4. The following are some of the causes of loss of body heat at night, and the methods of checking them:—

    (a) **By conduction.** When the body is lying on the ground much heat may be lost by conduction through the skin and ground. This especially applies if the ground or clothing are damp. It is usually better for men to lie on a ground sheet rather than use it as a covering.

    (b) **By evaporation.** When sweat is produced on the skin surface much loss of heat is caused by evaporation. Clothing which has become damp by sweating or rain, assists the conduction of heat out of the body, as mentioned above. Dry clothing with its minute air cells contained in the interstices of the material prevents loss of body heat; air being a bad heat conductor. It is important to prevent clothes becoming damp by sweat either during the day or before turning in at night. This can be partially achieved by removing as much clothing as practicable before commencing any extraordinary fatigue such as digging or climbing a steep obstacle, etc. It is a common fallacy to suppose that the greater the weight of a covering material the greater warmth retained. The warmest materials are those whose interstices, contains the largest number of air cells. Examples are, the lightweight camel-hair, angora, or wool blankets, which prove more satisfactory on a cold night than the heavy army type. String vests, on the same principle

of providing a layer of air, are warmer than the closely woven garments.

(c) **Through the lungs.** The loss of heat through the lungs is not automatically controlled. It occurs through evaporation on the surface of the membrane which lines the whole respiratory tract, and by conduction in the warming of each inspiration of air expired, with consequent loss of body heat.

This chilling through the lungs can be checked by breathing through a scarf or towel wrapped loosely round the face. In this way the evaporating power of the inspired air is reduced, and it is also warmed in its passage through the wool. This is a valuable aid in keeping warm on a cold night. It is not however recommended in sub-zero climates to breathe with the head inside the sleeping bag or blankets, lest the moisture produced by condensation should form a rime of frost inside.

5.   Training in hardening the body to exposure must be gradual. To begin with fires in huts and ante-rooms should be cut to a minimum and finally stopped altogether. Excess clothing such as unnecessary pullovers, waistcoats, long pants and overcoats should be gradually dispensed with. Cold showers, baths and all the year swimming should be encouraged. PT in all weathers, in trousers, socks and boots only should be carried out. Field service training should seldom be cancelled because of the weather. (This does not apply to Small Arms Training and Technical Training.) Men can become accustomed to a surprising degree of cold and exposure if they set their minds to it.

Resistance to Fatigue

6.   The training of muscles for unaccustomed stress cannot be achieved in less than a certain period of time, and whereas stiffness may be expected at the outset of training, it may retard rather than increase progress if carried too far. It is important to restrain the over enthusiastic officer or NCO who begins a new course of instruction by giving the men "a good shake up".

7.   Muscles which are unaccustomed to frequent usage may be strengthened and exercised by normal training carried out over the following types of country:—
> Heavy sodden marshy ground.
> Sandhills, beaches and dunes.
> Broken or ploughed ground.
> Hill country.
> Boulder land or rocky beaches.

8.   PT designed to toughen the body is adequately dealt with in the appropriate army manuals. (Also *see* "Mountain P.T." in Appendix D to MTP 90 Part III.)

Staleness

9.   Experiments have shown that elimination of salt from the diet produces lassitude and exhaustion. Strenuous training produces repeated and prolonged sweating with consequent loss of salt in the body. This salt must be replaced in food and drink. The best drink for men who are thirsty is a mug of water with a dash of oatmeal and a *pinch* of salt. The oatmeal makes the salt palatable.

10.   The nerves are also affected by increased physical endurance, the harder the physical work, the greater the output of energy from the nerves driving the muscles. The principal source of nutrition for the nerve centres is vitamin B1. The common sources of this are:—
> Peas and Beans.
> Eggs.
> Milk.
> Liver and offal.
> Wholemeal and oatmeal. (Army biscuit which is made
> of wholemeal is excellent food).

11.   Another principal cause of staleness is the mental factor. Mental effort is required all the time a man is driving his body to hard exercise, and a time may come during long periods of training when the will

power begins to fail from overwork. On long marches the dulling of the brain to a state of mental exhaustion may be offset by squad singing and simple observation exercises. Occasional days of physical rest are desirable, especially following a particularly strenuous day's exercise. Monotony of routine in camp and barrack life should be avoided, and in this respect the cinema can be usefully employed in the evening.

12.   Experience in the last war showed that men who suffered from fear in their first experience of combat, became so weak physically that they were unable to carry their individual loads. There is no set answer to this problem but a lot may be achieved by battle realism in field training, and this means more than mere lip service, and by the build-up of a man's esteem and self confidence by personal achievement.

13.   The answer to the question, how long does a man remain fit after strenuous training is discontinued, depends on the conditions under which he is living; amount of sleep; nervous strain; alcoholic and smoking habits; age and the degree of fitness reached. As a rough generalisation fitness begins to deteriorate rapidly after a week, and the longer period of inactivity the greater the time required to restore it. Strenuous exercise once a week is normally suitable for a moderate standard of fitness and men in such a condition should regain high peak in 7 to 14 days.

Living Out

14.   The problem facing the man is how to live as comfortably as possible in wet and cold conditions with only the protection of an anti-gas waterproof cape. The following general common sense notes may be of assistance to him:—

(a)   At the first opportunity dry all damp or wet clothing. Give the body a good rub down after any exercise involving sweating.

(b)   Wear the minimum amount of clothing before commencing violent exercise, in order to produce as little sweat as possible.

(c)   Dry newspaper or toilet papers packed carefully around the vital parts of the body (chest, kidneys and stomach) at night, help to retain body heat.

(d) A hot meal late at night or a hot drink should be taken to stoke up the temperature of the body. If possible have an additional garment to slip on in the chilly early hours.

(e) Take off damp or wet boots and stuff with paper. Rub the feet well with a rough cloth or battledress blouse and put into a pack or rucksack full of hay, dry grass, or even dry leaves.

(f) If possible sleep on the site of the fire for the evening meal, having raked away the dead embers.

(g) Always try to insulate the body from the ground by interposing cardboard, leaves, branches of fir' or spruce, dried dung, in fact anything that will prevent conduction of body heat into the ground.

(h) Wrap a towel, scarf or balaclava helmet around mouth and breath through it.

(i) Any form of muscular exercise produces heat in the body.

(j) Clothing should be worn loose and tight belts or puttees slackened before turning in.

Wind Breaks and Simple Bivouacs

15. It is seldom on active service that a man has time or opportunity to build an elaborate bivouac. The following basic principles will assist in giving him protection at night from the elements.

(a) Use a windbreak, either in its natural form such as a fallen tree or fold in the ground, or built artificially such as a sanger of stones, hole in the snow, or barricade of ration boxes.

(b) Within a section, if the tactical situation permits, rifle and bren groups should sleep herded together and thus benefit from the mutual body warmth provided.

(c) Cover from the weather may be obtained by use of the ground sheet or gas cape, either by the construction of lean-to or shelters, or by wrapping them around in the body. (*See* diagram 2).

(d) Snow shelters and igloos are described fully in MTP 90, Part V, Chapter 9.

Selection of Camp Sites

16.   The following essential points should be considered:—

    (a)   Wind—always blows up or down a valley; since the warm air tends to rise, the valley sides will be warmer than the valley bottom Cols or passes are particularly windswept.

    (b)   Shelter—trees, woods, gradual slopes or hills provide shelter. Camping in the lee of small obstructions, e.g., outcrops of rock, sometimes involves being exposed to draughts and air currents.

    (c)   Water—a natural water supply is a great advantage.

    (d)   Concealment—track discipline must be rigidly enforced. The outline of water proof cape bivouacs must be broken up with branches, scrim or local foliage. Every advantage should be taken of the natural shelter and camouflage afforded by woods and forests.

    (e)   Dispersion—is necessary as a means of protection from air attack. A normal guide is that the commander of a sub-unit should be able to exercise vocal control.

    (f)   Latrine and urinal trenches should be within the camp perimeter. Accidents occur when men wander outside the area at night.

    (g)   A good all round constantly manned observation post should be at hand even in supposedly safe areas.

Rations

17.   All ranks must understand that field rations for a special task are not a matter of like and dislike, but have to be devised scientifically to make good the particular losses the body will suffer. (*See* "Operational Feeding—Use of Special Ration Packs, 1943").

Cooking

18.   It is quicker and more economical if food is cooked on a group or sub-unit basis. Here teamwork is important and individual men

should carry out their chores without milling around and hindering the appointed cooks.

Compo foods are of a bland character, highly flavouring foods tiring the palate and producing dislike within a few days. However it is a good idea to carry small packets of seasoning such as sage, thyme, dried mint, onion flavouring and curry powder to make the "bully stew" more appealing to the appetite.

Training should incorporate instruction in cooking without utensils. Examples: Rabbit or wild bird, cleansed and covered with a layer of mud and inserted into the burning embers. Raw meat roasted on a sharp pointed stick over the fire.

Oatmeal is a useful easily carried basic food which can be prepared in many different ways, e.g., thickening stews or soups, porridge and "twists" made by rolling thin strips of oatmeal dough around a stick and inserting into the fire.

Eating on the March or during actual Operations

19.   Men should not over-eat at breakfast just before strenuous exertion. On the march small snacks of chocolate, biscuits, raisins or sweets should be eaten every hour or two, with a large hot meal if possible in the evening. Experience shows that men do not require very much food during the first 24–28 hours of an operation—and that generally they carry more food than ever required.

General Information on living in the Field

20.   Instructors are recommended to refer to the many excellent scouting manuals which although naturally of an elementary nature contain much information of value in bivouacing and camping.

APPENDIX E

STANDARDISED CLIFF ASSAULT PROCEDURE FOR TRAINING A COMMANDO TROOP

Introduction

1.   The drill is a training aid used to ensure that each man knows his job and others. Herein lies its danger and chief limitation. The drill can apply only to a standard cliff and standard circumstances, neither of which exist in practice. It must be varied and adapted to meet each cliff assault operation and exercise. It is important to emphasise that the drill must not be allowed to impose rigidity of thought or action. It is only a means to the end.

2.   The immediate aim is to transfer the force from its craft to an organised defensive cliff head position quickly, silently, securely and with the minimum disorganisation on the way.

Organisation

3.   When a Commando troop is employed in a cliff assault role certain adjustments have to be made to the organisation.

    (a)   The strength is reduced by having to provide numbers 1 and 2 climbers and covering parties who subsequently will form the cliff head defence party. They should include a bren group possibly from the troop support section.

    (b)   The PIAT or rocket launcher, and the 2in. mortar may not be required.[21]

---

[21]   Projector Infantry Anti-Tank (PIAT). A British standard issue World War II anti-tank weapon.

(c) A SNCO, usually the TQMS, is required as beach master and he needs a runner.[22]

(d) Bowmen must be appointed for each craft.

Equipment

4.

No. 1 Climbers	Pistol
	Knife
	$1\frac{1}{2}$in. Climbing rope coiled in a basket with one end tied round his waist, gripfast, earth axe.
	Grapnel and 30 foot knotted lin. line.
No. 2 Climbers	Sten
	Knife
	$1\frac{1}{2}$in. Climbing rope coiled in basket with one end tied round his waist, gripfast, earth axe.
	Grapnel and 30 foot knotted lin. line.
Beachmaster	Signalling torch.
Beachmaster's runner	Phone and cable coiled on a drum.
Troop Commander's runner	Phone (roped up with one end of wire attached to his waist).
Signallers	Sets as required.
Medical Orderly	Neil Robertson stretcher, First Aid Bag.
TSMs Runner	Carries 100 yards of white tape.

A roller, gripfast and snatch block, together with a 2in. or 2½in. rope for roller haulage are brought up by men detailed in the second wave.

PHASE I—The Sea Approach

5. A troop will normally land in two waves, the exact number in each wave depending on the type of craft used:—Dories, the 27ft. commando raiding craft or LCP(L).

---

[22] Senior Non-Commissioned Officer (SNCO) and Troop Quartermaster Sergeant (TQMS).

6.   The following should be in the first wave:—
       Troop commander and runner
       Cliff head officer
       TSM and runner [23]
       2 No. 1 climbers
       2 No. 2 climbers
       Beachmaster
       1 Signaller
       Port and starboard covering parties—each 1 NCO and 3
       Marines.

PHASE II—The Establishment of Ropes

7.   (a)   Bowmen hold craft in until cleared, meanwhile all make for
              the base of the cliff and select their routes to climb. No. 2's
              tend their ropes. Port and starboard covering parties take up
              fire positions to cover their respective flanks and the cliff top.

       (c)   The beachmaster makes a quick reconnaissance for the best
              landing points for the second wave. Boats return to their
              parent craft or lie off.

8.   (a)   Nos. 1 reach the cliff top, crawl over, secure their ropes and
              give two tugs. On receipt of this signal No. 2's rope up,
              pulling up their own ropes which they hand together with
              their gripfast to Nos. 1's. No. 2's cover No. 1's while the latter
              secure the second ropes. When the covering parties are up
              No. 2's move back the ropes to assist the others over the top.

       (b)   The covering parties are the next up, closely followed by the
              troop commander, the TSM, their runners and the signalmen.
              The first men have been holding the ends of No. 1's rope
              waiting for the two tugs signal showing that No. 2s' are up.
              It may be advisable if the cliff is loose for men to stay back
              under cover from falling stones. In this case a length of clean

---

[23]   Troop Sergeant Major (TSM).

white tape is tied to the ends of the A rope to show when the signal is given.

9.   (a) The covering parties cover their flanks; working in pairs and paying particular attention to any cliff path. Careful orders must lay down the section to be taken if individuals or a patrol approach and this action must be thoroughly rehearsed.

      (b) The troop commander selects a control point in the centre of the cliff head. If the assault is in darkness the TSM with his runner lays tape from the outermost gripfasts to this point.

      (c) The troop commander selects his sub-section positions and points them out to the TSM who is waiting at the troop HQ position. The latter then goes back to the control point ready to direct the second wave to their sub-section positions. The position now looks as given in Diagram 3.

10.   As soon as the troop commander is satisfied that all is going well he calls in the second wave by phoning to the beachmaster who uses his signalling torch. The phone and cable have been brought up by the troop commander's runner and is used in preference to wireless.

PHASE III—The Establishment of the Cliff Head Position

11.   Ideally the second wave should touch down as soon as the ropes are free so that the small vulnerable party at the top may be left alone no longer than can be avoided.

12.   The sub-section commanders are the first ashore and the first up. The remainder rush to the base of the cliff and there take up covering positions while waiting to rope up. The beachmaster keeps the ropes filled. On reaching the cliff top all men crawl over to avoid being silhouetted, and move forward until they reach the tape which they follow to the control point, where the TSM directs each man towards his own sub-section.

13.   As each sub-section is completed, sub-section commanders send their runners to report to the control point. The TSM reports the troop ready to the troop commander, while his runner takes up the tape.

14.   On this report the cliff head officer brings in the covering parties and numbers 1 and 2 climbers and moves them into the cliff head position.

15.   The troop is now ready to move off on the raid and the picture will look as given in Diagram 4.

16.   The cliff head party are left behind as a firm base to secure the line of withdrawal. The second signalman, with an 88 set, stays with the cliff head officer while the first moves off on the raid with the troop commander.

WITHDRAWAL

17.   While the raid is in progress the Leader No. 1 climber doubles his rope through the ring of his gripfast and camouflages the gripfast with turf. This rope will be used by the last man down.

18.   On return from the raid if the situation permits, the troop will take up cliff head positions as before. Runners are sent to the control point to report their sub-section in position. This will allow some re-organisation to take place and any casualties, stores or prisoners to be evacuated. In the event of a close pursuit or a running fight the troop will obviously pass through the cliff head position and get down as quickly as possible with any casualties.

19.   Assuming an orderly withdrawal, the troop commander will order PREPARE TO WITHDRAW. On this order the following action will take place:—

    (a)   The runner informs the beachmaster by phone and the beachmaster signals in the craft.

    (b)   No. 1 and No. 2 climbers go to the top of their ropes.

    (c)   Sub-section commanders send bren gunners to the cliff head party.

    (d)   The TSM, his runner and two signalmen rope down. The TSM establishes a control point on the beach. The others embark as soon as possible.

    (e)   The troop commander and his runner move to the control point on the cliff top.

20.   The troop commander then orders WITHDRAWAL. Sub-section commanders thin out their sub-sections and finally rope down themselves. Men waiting to descend hold the rope with one hand to tell when it is free, whereupon they immediately rope down. One subaltern is detailed to see, with the help of the No. 1 and 2 climbers, that all the ropes are kept filled.

21.   Sub-section commanders who are the last in their sub-section to descend, report to the TSM at the control point on the beach that all their sub-section are down.

22.   The troop commander then orders the cliff head party to thin out and withdraw, and ropes down himself followed by the No. 2 climbers.

23.   Finally the climbers untie the single ropes and let them go as they become free, the gripfast they fling out to sea in a previously picked position or secure them to their belts. The last man uses the double rope and on reaching the bottom hauls it through the ring of the camouflaged gripfast. This hidden piece of ironmongery is the only evidence left on the cliff top to show which way the raiders came or left. At the bottom ropes and equipment are gathered in hasty armfuls and all embark.

24.   Meanwhile the beachmaster has filled one boat at a time so that each can get away as quickly as possible. The frequently limited number of landing points make it imperative that each boat is withdrawn immediately it is fully loaded. All craft must be filled to maximum capacity in case any have been lost in the landing or subsequently; no attempt is made to fit men or equipment into the boats in which they landed or to load boats by sub-sections. The beachmaster, if the situation permits, makes a quick check that no ropes or other equipment is left on the foreshore before he re-embarks himself.

APPENDIX F

SPECIAL EQUIPMENT FOR COMMANDO AMPHIBIOUS ASSAULTS

PART I—CLIFF ASSAULT EQUIPMENT

The following list of equipment is to a scale suitable for a Commando Brigade. Stores of a consumable nature (such as rope) are included in quantity sufficient for a normal year's training and would suffice for at least two cliff assault operations and the training for them. Not all the items in the list are likely to be required in any assault.

2.　　Items marked NIV are not at present in the Naval Stores vocabulary or Army catalogue. Haulage stores are omitted from this list as they are included in Part II of this appendix.

Pattern No. or Catalogue No.	Description		Quantity
CD 1705	Nails Mugger	C	28 lbs.
CD 2960	Nails Edge with Screws and Stajples	C	4,000 No.
CD 2952	Nails Clinker Soft Alpine Pattern with Single Shank 1 x $1\frac{3}{8}$ inches	C	28 lbs.
CI 2967	Plate Heel Size " A " with Screws	C	75 prs.
CI 2968	Plate Heel Size " B " with Screws	C	75 prs.
NIV	Nails Tricounie No. 1	C	2,000 No.
AC 5025	Ropes Climbing 125 feet lengths	C	12 No.
AC 5274	Lines Alpine 200 feet lengths	C	25 No.
AC 5268	Karabiners (Spring Links)		75 No.

Pattern No. or Catalogue No.	Description		Quantity
AC 5256	Axes Ice with Ring and Sling		30 No.
AC 5021	Crampons Large		6 pts.
AC 5164	Crampons Small		6 prs.
AC 5165	Crampons Medium		12 prs.
AC 5266	Hammer Pitons		8 No.
AC 0215	Pitons 12-inch	C	25 No.
AC 0216	Pitons 16-inch	C	25 No.
AC 5150	Pitons	C	25 No.
AC 5151	Pitons	C	25 No.
AC 5152	Pitons		25 No.
AC 5153	Pitons	C	25 No.
WA 2820	Tape Tracing Beach-Head Mk 1	C	1,000 yds.
NIV	Ropes Nylon $1\frac{1}{4}$-inch	C	100 faths.
D5 C 1208	Cordage Manilla Hemp 1-inch	C	300 faths.
D5 C 1205	Cordage Manilla Hemp $1\frac{1}{2}$-inch	C	300 faths
D5 C 1207	Cordage Manilla Hemp 2-inch	C	200 faths.
D5 C 1209	Cordage Manilla Hemp $2\frac{1}{2}$-incli	C	100 faths.
NIV	Gripfast Medium		25 No.
NIV	Gripfast Small		25 No.
NIV	Grapnel Five Prong Light Throwing		25 No.
NIV	Rope Carrier Basket fitted with Shoulder Straps		20 No.
NIV	Gripfast Sand Large		4 No.
NIV	Grapnel 2-inch Mortar Bomb		36 No.
NIV	Grapnel 3-inch Martar Bomb		24 No.
NIV	Rope Box with Pin Case		8 No.
E12 475	Stretcher Neil Robertson		2 No.

Pattern No. or Catalogue No.	Description	Quantity
B8 5291	Snatch Block and Swivel Eye Shackle and Spring Forelock	4 No.
NIV	Headlight for Climbing	8 No.
NIV	Schermuly Rockets 6 lbs. Type B (Operational) fitted with grapnel head and complete with launchers	100 No.

NOTES:—

1. Consumable items are marked C.
2. The question of the incorporation of the special NIV stores into the Ratebook for Naval Stores is under consideration.

PART II—CLIFF HAULAGE EQUIPMENT

The following stores are on a scale suitable for the maintenance of one commando over cliffs. The stores for the "Roller" and "Bipod" methods are included since they will be used in the initial stages of an assault.

2.   Items marked NIV are not at present in the Naval Stores vocabulary or Army Catalogue.

ROLLER METHOD (Two Sets)

Pattern No. or Catalogue No.	Description	Quantity
NIV	Gripfasts Medium	4 Nos.
NIV	Haulage Roller	2 Nos.
B8 5219	Snatch Blocks $2\frac{1}{2}$-inch	2 Nos.
D5.C1207 (2-inch)	Cordage Manilla	As required;
D5 C1209 ($2\frac{1}{2}$-inch)		$2\frac{1}{2}$ times the height of the Cliff

BIPOD METHOD (One Set)

NIV	Gripfast Large (Sandfast) or OP Holdfast	1 No.
NIV	Gripfast Medium	3 No.
NIV	Haulage Roller	1 No.
NIV	Bipod	1 No.
AC 5268	Karabiners	6 No.
D5 C1207 (2-inch) D5 01209 ($2\frac{1}{2}$-inch)	Cordage Manilla	As required; 3 times the
D5 C1208	Cordage Manilla 1-inch	As required; 3 times the height of the Cliff
NIV	Traveller Haulage	1 No.
NIV	Strops 6-inch (Lineloops)	8 No

POWER HAULAGE

NIV	Sheers Tubular 2-inch	1 Set
5102A	Blocks Steel Snatch $2\frac{1}{2}$-inch	6 No.
	Holdfast Ordnance Pattern	3 No.
	Pickets	24 Nos.
N 21029	Anchors CQR 100 lbs.	2 No.
5101A	Blocks Steel Single 2-inch	6 No.
	Blocks and Tackle 2 x 2 inches	1 No.
NIV	Spreader Tubular 4 feet long x 2 inches	1 No.
(B5) N89	F SWR Extra Special 1-inch	1 Mile
C 1207	Cordage Manilla 2-inch (Haulage Rope)	2 Coils
C 1208	Cordage Manilla 1-inch (Return Rope)	2 Coils

5101	Blocks 1½-inch	2 No.
NIV	Rollers Haulage	2 No.
NIV	Power Winch	1 No.
C 3242	Cordage Sisal Tarred 1½-inch (Bacj Guy)	1 Coil
DHT 12-3	Hammers Ballpane 2 lbs.	1 No.
DHT 1617	Marlines Spikes 9-inch	2 No.
	Shackles 4-inch	2 No.
8719	Buoys Eliptical	2 No.
1251	Hammers Sledge 7 lb.	1 No.
1256	Hammers Sledge 14 lb.	1 No.
DUT 1829	Pliers Sidecutting 8-inch	1 No.
DHT 2419	Spanners Adjustable 6-inch	1 No.
	Spanners Plug	1 No.
	Oil HD 30	As required
	Gasoline	As required
C 1215	Cordage Manilla 4-inch Warps	10 faths.

NOTE:—The most suitable type of anchor depends on the sea-bed. The CQR is good except on rocky bottoms when the Danforth is recommended.

APPENDIX G

NOTES ON BOOTS AND OTHER FOOTWEAR FOR CLIMBING AND DIFFICULT LANDINGS

The conditions considered are:—
>Marching on roads.
>Marching across country.
>Night patrolling.
>Rock landings.
>Climbing as leader.
>Scaling with an established rope.
>Landing on quays and moles.

It will be appreciated that no one boot is likely to meet fully all these requirements, and even for one of them, some degree of compromise is necessary. It is therefore important to understand the characteristics of the various types of footwear available.

GS Boots (Boots Ankle)

2.   The boot is designed for marching on roads and general barrack and parade wear. It is light, hardwearing and offers reasonable support and protection to the feet. The hidden or flat nailing and the toe and heel plates are designed as a protection against wear rather than to prevent slipping, consequently the boot slips badly on mud, dry grass, rock or cobbles, making men clumsy and noisy, and incapable of silent movement at night. The toe plates are very dangerous for climbing: The boot is also supplied with a smooth rubber sole and heel suitable for patrolling (Boots Ankle Patrolling).

GS Boots with Vibram type Sole (Boots Special RM— formerly Boots SV)

3.   The vibram sole is used extensively in the Alps, nevertheless it is treacherous on wet rock if any trace of mud or vegetation is present (*see* Bulletin of the British Mountaineering Council for August 1950). It is therefore not suitable for leading on sea cliffs or landings: on wet rocks with seaweed, vegetation or mud on them. It is exceptionally good for road or cross-country marching and night work. Its long wearing qualities in general, campaigning are remarkable. It can reasonably be worn for scaling with an established rope when a slip is not fatal, provided the landing is not on slimy or seaweedy rock.

GS Boots with Triple Hob Nailing

4.   The toe plates are removed and the boot nailed with triple hobs. The boot is good for cross country work at night by preventing slipping, although on rock or road the nails are noisy. It is satisfactory but not silent for rock landings and scaling with a rope. It can be used by a climbing leader in an emergency but with considerably less efficiency than boots with correct climbing nailing. The nailing is heavier than of the standard GS boot, but lighter than climbing nailing.

GS Boot with Climbing Nailing

5.   The standard boot GS modified by removing the toe and heel plates and adding an extra clump sole can be nailed as a climbing boot. There are two main types of nailing:—
    (a)   Clinker nailing.
    (b)   Tricouni or other hard nailing.
    The principle of these nailings is that the soft clinker nail grips by allowing the rock to cut into it, while the hard tricouni grips by cutting into the rock. In theory therefore, the clinker should be used in hard rock and the tricouni in soft. In practice, hard rock is often covered by a surface of weather material, or deposits of earth, vegetation or seaweed. Hard nails,

cutting through this, obtain a good grip. Furthermore, the sharp points of hard nails can engage in minor rugosities and obtain an interlocking grip on small holds; the clinker being soft has to be rather large and cannot do so to the same degree. The points of the tricouni however become blunt by wear or heavy blows and may then become much less effective than an equally worn clinker; clinkers being large are heavier than tricouni.

6.   To sum up, tricouni nailing is in most circumstances better for cliff assault leaders, provided the nails are replaced when blunt. Clinker nailing is better for all round wear over a long period.

7.   Both types of climbing nailing are heavy, and may be noisy on rock or roads. They wear unduly if worn for marching on roads or in general wear and this should be avoided.

Boots climbing with Climbing Nailing (Boots Climbing)

8.   Boots climbing are of a better quality and more waterproof than GS boots and, not requiring an additional clump sole to take climbing nailing, are rather lighter and less clumsy when nailed. Otherwise the remarks at paras. 5, 6 and 7 above apply equally to them.

Gym Shoes

9.   Rubber soled gym shoes give an excellent grip on dry rock or stone but are dangerous on wet rock or stone. Being light they can be carried in the haversack or pocket for use for particular problems. They are silent at night but slippery in mud and so may cause floundering and noise. Unlike the vibram sole, a gym shoe can easily be wiped free of mud and water. It is of course useless for marching or other prolonged wear.

Felt and Rope Soles

10.   Felt soled boots were at one time supplied by Ordnance for patrol work and could be used to get a grip on wet dressed stone such as might

be found on a quayside, and on which nailed boots would slip. They are not at present in supply and would have to be specially manufactured. Rope soled shoes are sometimes used by rock climbers in place of rubbers for wet rock and would also be useful on wet dressed stone. Both types are unsuitable for marching or other prolonged wear as they wear out quickly and offer inadequate protection and support to the feet.

Use of Socks over Boots

11.   For particular operational problems or in a mountaineering mountaineering emergency, socks may be worn over boots. This will silence nailed boots and give vibram or other rubber soles some degree of grip on rock in wet muddy conditions.

Nomenclature

12.   Boot Ankle   CD 0035-71
                Boot Ankle Patrolling   CD 1851-78
                Boot RM Special   –
                Boot Climbing   CD 1765-72

APPENDIX H

NOTES ON THE ASSESSMENT OF CLIFFS FOR ASSAULT PURPOSES

In general terms the information required for cliff assault is:—

(a) **Landing Places**
Outlying rocks and navigational dangers.
Location of places at which landing craft can approach rook
State of sea.
Nature of rock shelf.
Holding ground.
Depth immediately off shore.

(b) **Cliffs**
Height.
Angle and changes in angle.
Nature of rock.
Location of shelves or easy pitches.
Cliff falls and paths.
Practicability for roping-up or scrambling.
Practicable climbs and routes.

2.   The means of obtaining information are:—

General Information
(a)   Intelligence reports including non-confidential coast reports.
(b)   Topographical maps and charts.

Geological Information
(c)   Geological maps and descriptive regional accounts.

Special Reports
(d)   Air Photography.
(e)   Agents' reports specially called for.
(f)   Reconnaissance.

3.   It will be appreciated that specially ordered reconnaissance will, if detected by the enemy, draw his attention unmistakably to the section of the coast concerned. The fact that the enemy gives no indication of detecting reconnaissance does not necessarily mean that he has not done so. It may be possible to cover reconnaissances by obtaining reports over considerable length of coast line. The cover will form part of the general security and deception plans, see Chapter 2 paragraph 15(b).

General Information

4.   General information is collected on the assumption that ports or beaches will be used: for landing and roads for movement inland. Reports do not therefore usually concern themselves greatly with cliffs or difficult coasts, except to warn the mariner to keep clear. of the latter. Nevertheless a considerable amount of general information may be collected from them. Navigational Coast Reports (Pilots) usually give definite information about, shelter from prevalent weather and often contain details of minor landing places or beaches. Intelligence reports, maps and charts are of course essential to the general planning of an operation and to the interpretation of the geologist and ad hoc information discussed below.

Geological Information

5.   Geological information is of first class importance:—
   (a) To enable an intelligent conjecture to be made as to the form of cliff likely to be found in an area.
   (b) To forecast the texture of the rock forming the cliff face, i.e. hard and sound, loose, or soft, etc.

6.   It is well however to appreciate that by itself geological information will not give a reliable forecast of the practicability of cliffs for climbing or assault, and air or other photographs are required to establish the shape of a given cliff. The problem is authoritatively described thus:—
   "… the forms of cliffs are infinite. The chief formative factors are the nature of the rocks, which may be hard or soft, finely or

massively bedded; the inclination of the strata composing the cliff, which may be horizontal or directed seaward or landward; and the topography of the land into which the sea is cutting, which may be gently sloping upland, a country diversified with many small valleys or an area of boulder clay. The degree of exposure and the size and force of the waves acting upon it are also important."

"Coastline of England and Wales" —J. A. Steers

7.   Subject to the above, the following classification has been found useful.

(a)   **Igneous Rock** (*especially granite and gabbro*)
        Examples:—Lands End—Granite, good.
                Bullers of Buchan, Peterhead—Granite partly decomposed.
                Botallack Head, Cornwall—Gabbro.

        Except in the case of decomposed rock, the cliffs are steep but the rock is safe, giving good rock climbing of the type approved by the mountaineer. Granites however differ much in their characteristics. Some weather poorly and form much rubbly ground. A confident deduction cannot therefore be made from the fact that a coastline is mapped as granite. Most rocks of the gabbro type are however good for climbing. Operationally the climbs can often be avoided by using scramble routes around them Landing is usually easy on the rocks at the foot of the cliffs, but outlying rocks may be dangerous, especially at night or if a sea is running. Hard igneous rocks often form headlands on a coastline of softer rock.

(b)   **Gneisses and Schists**
        Examples:—Cape Wrath—Gneiss.
                Bolt Head and Start Point—Schists.

        Gneisses may be roughly classed with igneous rock for assault purposes. Mica schist and quartzitic schists often form somewhat less bold cliffs. The rock is climbable if carefully and sensibly used; the holds, not having the unfailing certainty associated with the best types of igneous rocks, should be tested before use. Hornblende schist is often extremely rotten and treacherous.

(c) **Slates, Shales and Grits**
Example:—North and South Devon Coasts.

These are a very common type of coastline but the cliffs are very unsatisfactory and dangerous to climb. The coast often runs to low points at the headlands with high "quarry" type cliffs between them, these latter cliffs being often unclimbable. Between the headlands there are often beaches, the larger ones with roads, the smaller ones sometimes with fishermans paths. KM Landing will be on the long points running out to sea from the headlands, but sometimes continue in shallow rocky reefs which are impossible for landing in a seaway.

(d) **Limestone (excluding chalk)**
Example:—Gower Peninsular, Pembrokeshire.

Limestone coasts are very distinctive. The cliffs are often high and continuous but sometimes sloping at about 45 degrees. Where climbable they are very spectacular although not necessarily difficult; but high and overhanging cliffs may make climbing or scaling impracticable. Holds are usually fairly sound but should be treated with suspicion. The rock may be very slippery between tidemarks.

(e) **Sandstone**
Example:—Coast on both sides of mouth of River Exe.

Varies very greatly in degree of cementation. Cliffs tend to be fairly steep; holds on hard sandstone may be sound (e.g., Harrison's Rocks in Kent), but other wise it may have to be treated similarly to chalk.

(f) **Chalk**
Example:—Deal and Dover Coastline.

High, steep and unbroken cliffs are very typical of chalk and tend to be unclimbable. Rockets carrying ladders were used during World War II on vertical chalk, but the height over which this method can be used is limited. Where the sea is prevented from washing away the debris, falls of rock may leave slopes in gulleys and ramps which are possible for roping up with a rocket or mortar line, climbing by step cutting, or scrambling. Beaches appear to be common at the foot of these cliffs.

(g) **Clay, and Sand**
Example:—Suffolk and Solent Coastlines.

These present a real, if not very spectacular, obstacle. Step cutting or a line firing mortar should deal with them without difficulty. Superficial slipping is a feature of many cliffs composed of alternation of clay and sand. This gives rise to a mass of disintegrating and slipping material in a state of instability or of actual movement, forming an almost impassable apron of mud. It is well illustrated by Fairlight Cliffs at Hastings.

Another common form of coastal cliff consists of alternating hard and soft strata, e.g., bands of varying thickness composed of limestone, sandstone, sandy shale and shale. Such cliffs are usually easy to scale if the component of dip of the strata on the cliff face is reasonably low, say less than 15°, and if there is no component of dip in the direction outwards from the cliff face. Otherwise such cliffs may be difficult or impossible to climb. The Yorkshire coast near Whitby shows good examples.

8.   In planning cliff assault, the advice of a trained geologist should be sought, as the subject requires prolonged training and experience to master. Nevertheless, officers and cliff leaders should be trained in the elements of geology so that they can make best use of expert advice and apply it to the particular problems of cliff assault with which geological experts are not likely to be familiar. Officers should also know how to obtain and use basic geological information if no expert advice is available to them.

Special Reports

9.   Large scale (1:10,000 or over) oblique and vertical air photographs are of very great: value and almost essential. Obliques should be used in assessing rock faces and should if possible include some having the

headlands in profile from which the slope. can be estimated. Verticals are required for planning sea approaches, landing places and routes on cliffs. They do not of course show the cliff face but give a clear indication of areas in which the slope is considerably less than vertical.

10.   It is not always possible to choose a climbing route from air photographs and guarantee that it will go. Given the air photographs, the angle to the vertical, and type of rock, it is usually possible however to say that practicable climbs will occur in a certain area and certain features and routes are indicated as possible first choices. Assessment of unknown cliffs on these lines, checked by visits and detail trials of climbs, are part of the training of officers and cliff leaders.

11.   Accurately timed air photographs taken at low water and other known stages of the tide are particularly valuable.

Agents' Reports

12.   It is not easy for a non-climber to estimate the possibility of climbing cliffs; a. mountaineer could give valuable information, but even he would be unreliable on troop practibility. Therefore, agents should be asked for the definite facts enumerated in paragraph 1 above. Photographs, including those showing the profile would be useful, and details of enemy dispositions will of course be included as in any other intelligence report.

Canoe Reconnaissance

13.   Subject to security considerations, canoe reconnaissance, allowing proposed landing and climbing places to be visited and possibly tested, should produce reports of a considerable degree of reliability. Each canoe should have at least one experienced cliff leader, the other member of the canoe being an experienced canoeist. Definite tasks should be allotted in briefing and the men making the reconnaissance interrogated as soon as possible after their return. Briefing and interrogation should

be carried out by an officer experienced in cliff assault, who should have air photographs on which to brief and interrogate. Canoeists are unlikely to be able to give their reports in general terms as they will be unable to obtain a wide view of the cliffs. They should therefore be ordered to locate and report on definite landing places, climbs, etc.

14.   A periscope reconnaissance may be possible by daylight which will give a more general view of the coast and enable plans and canoeists reports to be made into a complete picture.[24]

---

[24]   During World War II, this type of specialist work was conducted by Combined Operations Pilotage Parties (COPPs). Each team comprised members drawn from the Royal Navy and British Army. Their primary task was to conduct covert beach reconnaissance.

APPENDIX I
CLIFF HAULAGE METHODS

There are three main methods of hoisting stores to the top of cliffs. These are described in detail in the following paragraphs.

(a) **Roller Method.** This consists of fixing a light roller to the edge of the cliff and hauling up men carrying loads on their backs. These men use their feet to keep themselves and their loads off the cliff face. The hauling is done by a team of eight to twelve men on the cliff top and this exhausting work naturally puts a limit on the rate and extent of supply. Generally speaking this method is suitable for small scale raids or the assault stage of larger operations. 3in. mortars and ammunition can be hauled up by this method. A landing ledge or beach is necessary as it is seldom practicable to haul the load carriers direct out of the boat.

(b) **Bipod Method.** In this method a light metal sheerleg is erected on the cliff edge. A standing line is run from its head to the beach or to an anchor on the sea bed off shore. Travellers attached to the ha ulage line are fixed to the standing line and loads hauled up by man power from the beach or craft. Slightly larger loads can be handled this way than by the roller method described above but it suffers from the same limitations as to rate and extent of supply and is equally uneconomical in manpower. It has however the great advantage that loads can be hoisted directly from craft off shore which do not have to beach or attempt difficult landing. This can be done with training in a swell of six feet. This method is useful for troop or company scale raids and as a supplement to power haulage described below, particularly in the evacuation of casualties.

(c)   **Power operated.** This method is substantially the same as above except a stronger sheerlegs is used and a petrol motor substituted for the haulage team. The motor can be hoisted up by hand, followed by its light platform and connected to run up an endless haulage line. To this line is attached two or more slings or hooks for the loads. By this means a rate of supply of five to eight tons an hour can be achieved, depending on the height of the cliff. Loads of up to 4cwt can be hoisted from the beach or craft off shore. This method has every advantage over the one previously described and should enable forces of some strength to be maintained for considerable periods, especially if several sheerlegs and ropeways are used. It does however take nearly an hour to set up.

ROLLER METHOD—*See* Diagram 5

2.   The roller is attached to the back of a man who ropes up a rope established by a climber or by projection methods. It is then fixed so that if possible it just protrudes over the edge of the cliff. It is anchored to a gripfast placed a yard or two back. *See* Diagram 5.

3.   No. 2 of the team carries up the haulage rope (2 to 2½ in.) and a snatch block using a gripfast (or two if necessary) so that the haulage team can pull along level ground and not uphill. A minimum of six men are required as "mules" on an average cliff.

4.   A bowline of the bight is made at the end of the haulage rope and the carriers put a leg through each bight and hold the rope with both hands fairly low down. On being hauled up they fend themselves off the cliff by the use of their legs.

5.   Carriers Manpack have proved the most suitable load carriers.

Casualty Evacuation

6.   It is possible to evacuate casualties by using this method in reverse. The casualty is placed in a bag with holes for his legs and harness for attachment to the back of his escort. If possible he eases his weight on his escorts back by holding the haulage rope. The escort with his legs in the double bowline is then lowered slowly down the cliff with the casualty on his back.

7.   A casualty in a Neill Robertson stretcher may be escorted down the cliff by the following means. The haulage rope is attached to the ring at the head of the stretcher leaving a six foot tail which the escort ties round his waist as a safety measure. The escort now attaches himself tightly to the stretcher with his line loop and lets himself be lowered slowly down the cliff by the "mules". He leans out at right angle to the cliff and holds the stretcher away from the rock. This is the simplest method of casualty evacuation for seriously wounded men.

BIPOD METHOD—*See* Diagrams 6 and 7

8.   This method consists essentially of 2in. rope stretched taut from top to bottom of the cliff at an angle of approximately 30°. The loads are hooked on to this cable by karabiners or attached to a traveller and hauled up by hand with a 1in. rope.

9.   The haulage team consist of 1 NCO and 6 Marines carrying the following equipment:—

NCO i/c	Roller, gripfast, snatch block, 3 karabiners	⎫
No. 1	Bipod, gripfast, 3 karabiners	
No. 2	2in. haulage rope, gripfast, 3 karabiners	⎬ Cliff top party
No. 3	Haulage line	⎭
No. 4	Sand gripfast or OP holdfast	⎫
No. 5	Traveller	⎬ Beach or Boat Party
No. 6		⎭

Beach to Cliff Top—*See* Diagram 6

10.   The equipment is erected in the following sequence:—

(a)   The NCO i/c ropes up one of the previously established ropes carrying on his back a roller and a gripfast. On reaching the cliff top he decides on the most suitable site for the haulage point, and then puts the roller on the cliff edge and secures it by the gripfast. If by day he then signals to the remainder of the party by raising both arms above his head to show the proposed position of the bipod. At night he makes his way back to the ropes and collects the remainder of his party and leads them to the selected site.

(b)   No. 1 ropes up with the bipod lashed to his back with the points uppermost. He then makes his way to the site and erects the bipod in the position indicated by the NCO i/c.

(c)   No. 2 ropes up with a gripfast and one end of the 2in. rope. This rope having previously been flaked out on the beach by Nos. 4 and 5 so that it will run out freely clear of snags. Nos. 2 and 5 then work together flicking the rope along the cliff edge to the proposed site. The rope is next run through the link in the top of the bipod, and back inland about 10 yards where the gripfast is put in and a turn is taken with the rope. About 5 yards of the rope end should remain.

(d)   No. 3 ropes up with a gripfast and one end of the lin. rope, No. 6 having previously flaked out this rope on the beach to ensure that it will run freely. No. 3 and 6 then flick the rope along the cliff edge to the site. The second gripfast is then put in about 5 yards inland of the first and both ropes are secured to it by a round turn and two half hitches. No. 3 then secures the lin. rope to the top of the bipod straining it taut so as to act as a back guy.

(e)   As soon as both ropes are secured as given above, the NCO i/c signals to the beach party, giving two distinct tugs on each rope,

(f)   The beach party assists the cliff top party as stated above in establishing the two ropes, in addition they select and

establish the bottom anchor. This may be any one of the following:—

   (i) A convenient rock or boulder belay with a rope strop and karabiner.
   (ii) Sandfast either used normally or turned upside down and piled with rocks or boulders.
   (iii) O.P driven into the beach.
   (iv) 6ft. length of 2in. water pipe buried to a depth of 2ft. (across the line of pull).

(g) As soon as the two tug signals are received on the 2in. rope the slack is run down and the rope tautened by means of a haulage knot (Diagram 8). The haulage traveller is then put on the taut rope, and the 1in. rope tied to its top end.

(h) If there is no traveller available, as soon as the tug signals are received on the 1in. rope two figures of eight knots are made about 6ft. apart, each knot making a loop about 3in. long. Each of these loops is then hooked to the 2in. rope by karabiner.

Craft to Cliff Top—*See* Diagram 7

11.   If there is no beach or rock ledge the haulage may be set up direct from the sea to the cliff top. The main differences are as follows:—

(a) The haulage knot for setting up the 2in. rope is at the cliff top.
(b) The bottom anchor is replaced by two kedge anchors laid out with approximately 60° between the two warps.
(c) The craft is made fast to the 2in. rope by bow and stern lines which have a karabiner at the ends. This enables the craft to move backwards and forwards along the 2in. rope to suit the height of tide, swell, etc.

Casualty Evacuation

12.   The casualty, in a Neil Robertson stretcher, is attached to the traveller or by karabiners to the taut rope and lowered gently down.

POWER OPERATED SHEERLEGS METHOD.—*See* Diagrams 8, 9 and 10

General

13. This method consists of a double BLONDIN. WIRE operated by a petrol driven winch unit. It is normally erected from sea bed to cliff top in order that stores may be hoisted from the craft; it can however be set up from beach to cliff top.

Craft to Cliff Top

14.   Personnel required.

The team necessary to erect the equipment consists of an officer, SNCO and To Marines. The operating team consists of a NCO and 5 Marines.

Officer/SNCO Comd ⎰ Cliff top party
Nos. 1–6   ⎱
Nos. 7–10   Craft party

Equipment

15.   The stores are laid out in the craft so that they are ready to land. The 1in. Extra Special Flexible Steel Wire Rope, 2in. and 1in. ropes are all wound on to drums so that they will run freely. The wire is first middled and the two ends brought together, both traveller blocks are fed on and run to the top of the bight and secured with a lashing. The two ends of the wire are shackled together and fed on to the drum first so that the bight and traveller blocks are on top.

Sequence of Erection

16.   *(a)*   The craft approaches the selected area, and drops its kedge. A second craft takes in a bow line to the rock ledge, or lays out a second forward. These warps are then adjusted till the first craft lies as close to the rocks as is safe with existing sea conditions.

(b)   The cliff top party are ferried in to the rock ledge taking the following loads.

Comd	OP Holdfast
No. 1	8 OP Holdfast, Pickets, and 7lb. Sledge Hammer.
No. 2	One end of 2in. haulage rope (the other end attached to bight of ESFSWR), both travellers ready on wire and secure in end of bight.
No. 3	2in. Double-double tensioning tackle.
No. 4	6 OP Holdfast pickets, lashing and 2½in. snatch block.
No. 5	3in. snatch block, 1½ in. single back guy.
No. 6	Roller and Medium Gripfast.

(c)   The cliff top party then rope up or are hauled up the cliff by roller method.

(d)   (i) Comd. and No. 1 drive in the OP Holdfast approximately 30 yards inland of the selected site.

       (ii) Nos. 2 and 6 haul up 2in. rope and wire bight. (Nos. 6 having previously positioned roller with grip fast). The ends of the 2in. haulage rope are then secured to both travellers as shown in the diagrams; the length of the 2in. rope being estimated to meet all conditions, and the bight, snatched into the 2½in. snatch block, positioned by No. 4.

The ends of the 2in. haulage rope are then secured to both travellers as shown in diagrams; the length of the 2in. rope being estimated to meet all conditions, and the bight snatched into the 2½in. snatch block, positioned by No. 4.

       (iii) Nos. 3 and 5 unstrap tackle, overhauling if necessary. Hook on to anchor and shackle on 3in. snatch block.

       (iv) No. 4 drives in anchor and secured 2½in. snatch block.

(e)   (i) Nos. 7 and 8 pay out 2in. haulage rope until the end is reached. The wire bight and travellers are then secured and paid out.

(ii) Nos. 9 and 10 prepare the kedges and warps and pass them into the kedge dory.

(iii) As soon as the comd signals that the wire is secured at the top, the end of the wire is transferred to the craft, leaving the drum aboard. The spreader in the meantime is fixed between the two wires and the first kedge warp bent on.

(iv) The craft them moves out to sea towing out the remainder of the wire. The craft proceeds until the wires and the kedge warp are strained as tight as possible, the first kedge anchor is let go. The craft then returns and picks up the wire and traces it back to the shackle. The second kedge anchor is bent on and laid out at approximately 60° to the first, swinging the wire as taut as possible. As soon as the comd sees the second kedge dropped he orders his party to tension up using the tackle.

(f) The traveller is then lowered down the wire to the craft and one end of the lin. return rope is secured to the self mousing block on the traveller. The sheerleg moves upwards, the other traveller is allowed to go down to the craft. On reaching the craft, the other end of the lin. return rope is secured to the self mousing block, and adjusted for length. The bight is then passed through 2 snatch blocks, which are secured fore and aft in the craft. Details of a traveller are shown in Diagram 11.

(g) The remaining cliff top stores as listed below are then hauled up and erected as shown in the diagram.

Power Winch Unit

OP Holdfasts and Pickets.

Method of Operation

17. (a) The operating team consists of:—

NCO (Comd)
No. 1 (Winch Driver) ⎫ Cliff Top
No. 2 and 3 (unloading) ⎬
                        ⎭
Nos. 7 and 8 (loading)   Craft Party

(b) The winch motor is started up and the first stores craft brought alongside the haulage craft.

(c) Three turns are then taken round the winch drum and the first load hooked on. As soon as the signal to hoist is given, the winch driver throttles up and lets in the clutch. When the load reaches the top the clutch is slipped out and the load is unhooked. By this time the other traveller will have reached the craft. The second load is hooked on and the turns on the winch drum reversed. The clutch is then let in as before and the operation repeated until the craft is cleared of stores.

(d) This equipment takes 45–60 minutes to erect, and once erected will deliver stores at a rate of 6–8 tons per hour.

Beach to Cliff Top—*See* Diagram 10

18.   If the beach, or rock ledge at the foot of the cliff is suitable this equipment can be erected from the beach to cliff top as shown in Diagram 10. The main differences are as follows:—

(a) The tensioning tackle is at the bottom.

(b) The power winch is at the bottom.

(c) In this set up, both return and haulage ropes should be 2in. cordage and travellers constructed as for craft to cliff top.

Sketch 1

Note:– It is useful to carry a few nails in the pack.

A simple lean-to made by utilising a fallen tree, hedge or wall as one side of the bivouac.

Sketch 2

One of the open ends of the two man bivouac should be sealed with sods of earth or stones and mud.

Sketch 3

The gas cape is worn normally and the waterproof cape is bound together through the holes and around the legs, making a parcel of the feet. This measure is both effective and warm, but its use depends on the tactical situation.

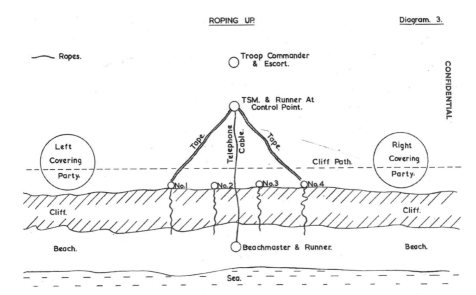

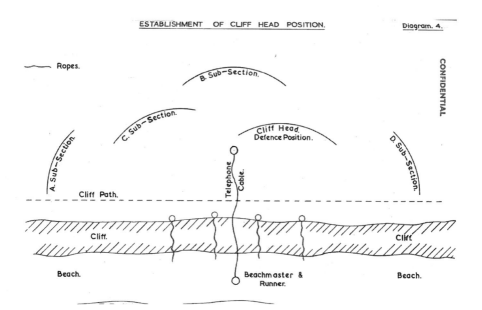

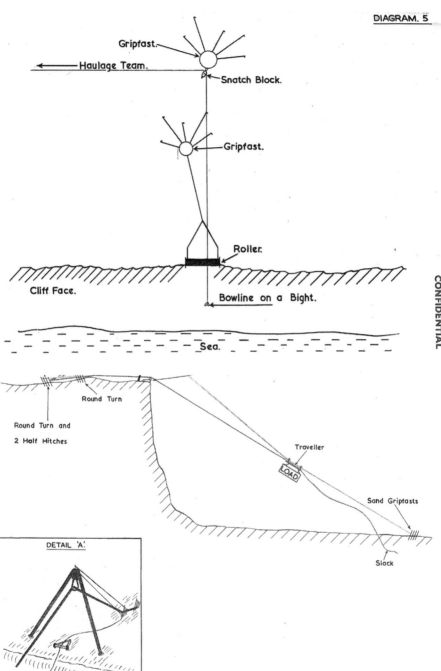

CONFIDENTIAL

DIAGRAM. 5

Gripfast.

Haulage Team.

Snatch Block.

Gripfast.

Roller.

Cliff Face.

Bowline on a Bight.

Sea.

Round Turn

Round Turn and
2 Half Hitches

Traveller

LOAD

Sand Gripfasts

Slack

DETAIL 'A'.

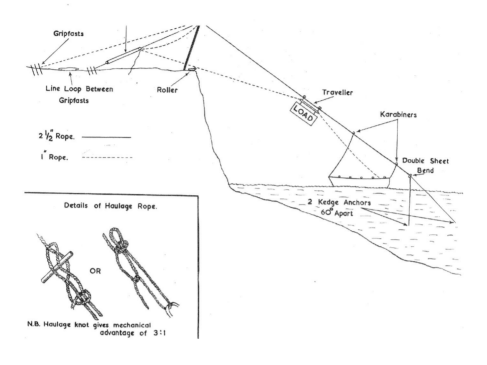

Gripfasts

Line Loop Between Gripfasts

Roller

Traveller

LOAD

Karabiners

Double Sheet Bend

2 Kedge Anchors 60° Apart

2 ½" Rope. ————

1" Rope. - - - - - - -

Details of Haulage Rope.

OR

N.B. Haulage knot gives mechanical advantage of 3:1

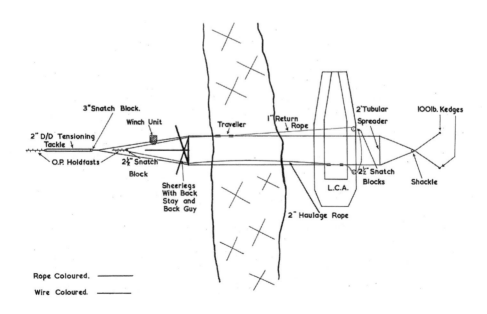

3" Snatch Block.

Winch Unit

Traveller

1" Return Rope

2' Tubular Spreader

100lb. Kedges

2" D/D Tensioning Tackle

O.P. Holdfasts

2½" Snatch Block

Sheerlegs With Back Stay and Back Guy

2½" Snatch Blocks

L.C.A.

Shackle

2" Haulage Rope

Rope Coloured. ————

Wire Coloured. ————

CONFIDENTIAL

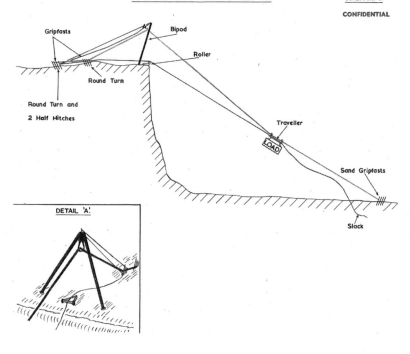

Gripfasts

Bipod

Roller

Round Turn

Round Turn and
2 Half Hitches

Traveller

LOAD

Sand Gripfasts

Slack

DETAIL 'A!

CONFIDENTIAL

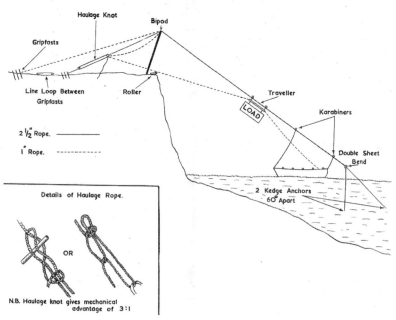

Haulage Knot

Bipod

Gripfasts

Line Loop Between
Gripfasts

Roller

2 ½" Rope. —————

I" Rope. -- -- -- --

Traveller

LOAD

Karabiners

Double Sheet
Bend

2 Kedge Anchors
60° Apart

Details of Haulage Rope.

OR

N.B. Haulage knot gives mechanical
advantage of 3:1

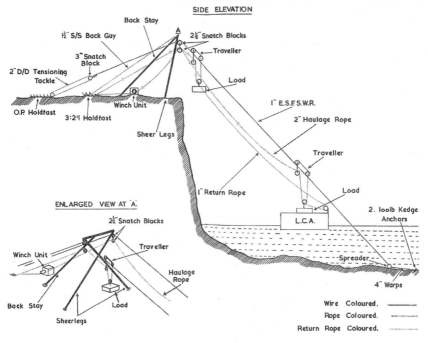

Back Stay

1½" S/S Back Guy

A

2½" Snatch Blocks

Traveller

3" Snatch Block

2" D/D Tensioning Tackle

Load

O.P. Holdfast

Winch Unit

3:2" Holdfast

Sheer Legs

1" E.S.F.S.W.R.

2" Haulage Rope

Traveller

Load

1" Return Rope

L.C.A.

2. 100lb Kedge Anchors

Spreader

4" Warps

ENLARGED VIEW AT 'A'.

2½" Snatch Blocks

Winch Unit

Traveller

Haulage Rope

Back Stay

Load

Sheerlegs

Wire Coloured. ————

Rope Coloured. ————

Return Rope Coloured. ————

POWER OPERATED SHEERLEGS METHOD

CRAFT TO CLIFF TOP

PLAN.

DIAGRAM. 9.

CONFIDENTIAL

3" Snatch Block.

Winch Unit

Traveller

1" Return Rope

2' Tubular Spreader

100lb. Kedges

2" D/D Tensioning Tackle

O.P. Holdfasts

2½" Snatch Block

Sheerlegs With Back Stay and Back Guy

L.C.A.

2½" Snatch Blocks

Shackle

2" Haulage Rope

Rope Coloured. ————

Wire Coloured. ————

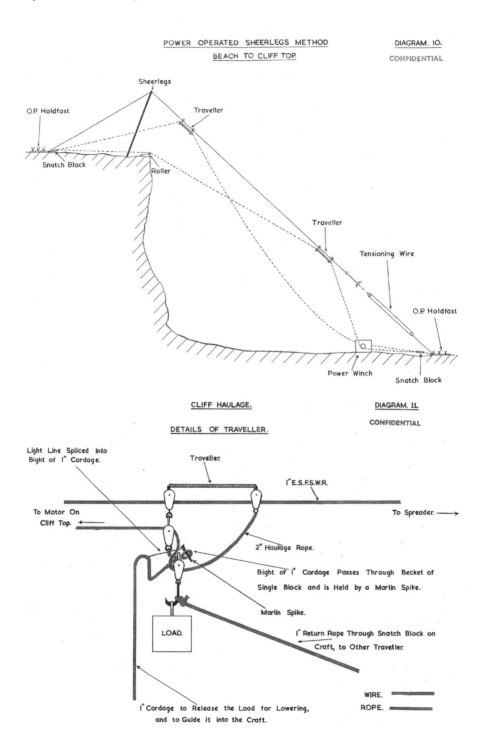

POWER OPERATED SHEERLEGS METHOD
BEACH TO CLIFF TOP

DIAGRAM. 10.
CONFIDENTIAL

Sheerlegs

O.P. Holdfast

Traveller

Snatch Block

Roller

Traveller

Tensioning Wire

O.P. Holdfast

Power Winch

Snatch Block

CLIFF HAULAGE.

DETAILS OF TRAVELLER.

DIAGRAM. 11.
CONFIDENTIAL

Light Line Spliced Into
Bight of 1" Cordage.

Traveller.

1" E.S.F.S.W.R.

To Motor On
Cliff Top.

To Spreader.

2" Haulage Rope.

Bight of 1" Cordage Passes Through Becket of
Single Block and is Held by a Marlin Spike.

Marlin Spike.

LOAD.

1" Return Rope Through Snatch Block on
Craft, to Other Traveller.

1" Cordage to Release the Load for Lowering,
and to Guide it into the Craft.

WIRE.

ROPE.

Appendix: Definition of a Royal Marines Commando

"A Royal Marines Commando is trained, equipped and supported beyond conventional forces to operate in all environments and deliver mission success against the most challenging military imperatives."

Company Sergeant Major Tony Wilson RM, May 2020

Qualities/Characteristics

- Not a "yes" man or a "creeper". A Royal Marines Commando should be his own man and not a careerist eager to please senior officers. Such men were RTU'd by wartime Commando units
- Never turns a blind eye, but speaks truth to power
- Treats others with dignity and is driven to make a difference for the better
- Possesses the moral courage and integrity always to do the right thing
- Prizes loyalty, selflessness, self-discipline, humility and understated excellence.
- Knows himself, and above all his own weaknesses
- Has the ability to think at least two ranks above his own
- Highly individualistic but able to operate as a key member of a high-functioning team
- Possesses an above average level of intelligence
- Mentally and physically fit and robust and possessed of an ability to surpass his own mental and physical limitations
- Possessed of a keen sense of humour
- Possessed of emotional intelligence
- Has "street sense": common sense "with an edge"

- A Commando must possess a healthy dose of scepticism, a driven sense of adventure, and no small measure of a mischievous nature
- Adaptable, versatile, flexible, innovative and never gives up
- Possessed of "extreme pragmatism" and stubbornness
- An ability to minimize or circumvent staff work and stifling bureaucracy, as well as simplify the complex and be able to communicate this effectively
- An ability not only to change the atmospherics of a situation, but also its dynamics
- An ability to "know his enemy", think like him and, where appropriate, act like him

Mind–Set

- A soldier for "all seasons" with the capability to operate anywhere in the world, in any environment, or climate
- Understands and respects military operations as but one element of a larger jigsaw
- Keenly interested in the world
- Seeks a deep understanding of his operating environment, the enemy and the people
- Thinks clearly and humanely, even in adversity, when degraded, angry or afraid
- Places the mission first, the team second and himself third.
- Must be audacious and entertain an increased, but balanced, level of risk to life to reduce risk to mission success
- The ability to endure hardship and still fully function
- Thrives in chaos and ambiguity and has the judgement to balance risk versus reward
- The ability to take-on a near peer or peer adversary who enjoys a three-to-one force ratio advantage

Training/Skill-sets

- Trained alongside all ranks, egalitarian by outlook, to include valuing the ideas of everyone
- Highly trained in amphibious/littoral strike operations
- Highly trained in mountain and arctic warfare
- Highly trained in jungle and urban fighting
- An expert at camouflage and concealment, stealth and deception
- A first-class marksman, expert in close quarter tactics and CQ Marksmanship
- Knowledgeable of, and skilled at, operating weapon systems employed by opponent forces at the tactical level
- Expert at demolitions and unarmed combat, as well as Methods of Entry trained
- Parachute trained
- Just as highly competent in waging medium-level, high-intensity wars, as in operating in specialist, sub-threshold theatres against non-state actors
- The ability to master and utilise emerging technologies but not become their servant
- A first-class, specialised amphibious infantryman. Field Marshal Sir Archibald Wavell once defined the ideal infantryman as a "mixture of cat-burglar, poacher and gunman"[238]